The Young Writer's Craft

For Ann,

with many thanks
for your insights
& thoughts —
& with best wishes
Valerie Thornton for good health.

Valerie Thornton

March 2011

HODDER
GIBSON
PART OF HACHETTE LIVRE UK

The Publishers would like to thank the following for permission to reproduce copyright material:
Photo credits Page 1 © Elena Butinova – Fotolia.com; Page 3 ICP / Alamy; Page 59 FLPA/Terry Whittaker; Page 79 Hodder Gibson; Page 81 Jean Van Starten/Jupiter Images; Page 99 David Paterson / Alamy; Page 103 © Valerie Thornton; Page 117 imagebroker / Alamy; Page 151 © Valerie Thornton; Page 187 Melvin Grey /NHPA/Photoshot; Page 204 © Kerioak – Fotolia.com. All other photographs © Valerie Thornton.
Acknowledgements 'in the beginning' by Tom Leonard is reproduced with permission of the author; 'Age Concern' © Teresa McCluskey. This poem appeared in *Beneath the Waterfall*, an anthology of work by Hieton Writers Group (2005); 'Red Deer' and 'Clydesdale' from *Collected Poems* by Edwin Morgan, published by Carcanet Press Limited (1995); 'Tigger' © Anne Donovan, originally written for BBC Radio Scotland Education; 'Easter Eggs' © Anne MacLeod; 'All That Glitters' © Carolyn Mack; 'An Eye for an Eye' © Maureen Sullivan; 'Moon-Ravens' from *Collected Poems for Children* by Ted Hughes is reproduced by permission of Faber and Faber Ltd; 'Fahim 911' was written by Evelyn Jean-Louis for the Open University A174 Start Writing Fiction Course; 'A Symbol of Hope' is reproduced with permission of The Western Education and Library Board, Northern Ireland.
Every effort has been made to trace all copyright holders, but if any have been inadvertently overlooked the Publishers will be pleased to make the necessary arrangements at the first opportunity.

Although every effort has been made to ensure that website addresses are correct at time of going to press, Hodder Gibson cannot be held responsible for the content of any website mentioned in this book. It is sometimes possible to find a relocated web page by typing in the address of the home page for a website in the URL window of your browser.

Hachette's policy is to use papers that are natural, renewable and recyclable products and made from wood grown in sustainable forests. The logging and manufacturing processes are expected to conform to the environmental regulations of the country of origin.

Orders: please contact Bookpoint Ltd, 130 Milton Park, Abingdon, Oxon OX14 4SB. Telephone: (44) 01235 827720. Fax: (44) 01235 400454. Lines are open 9.00–5.00, Monday to Saturday, with a 24-hour message answering service. Visit our website at www.hoddereducation.co.uk. Hodder Gibson can be contacted direct on: Tel: 0141 848 1609; Fax: 0141 889 6315; email: hoddergibson@hodder.co.uk

First published in 2008 by
Hodder Gibson, an imprint of Hodder Education, an Hachette Livre UK Company,
2a Christie Street
Paisley PA1 1NB

ISBN-13: 978 0340 966 549

Impression number   5 4 3 2 1
Year   2012 2011 2010 2009 2008

Cover photo © Stockbyte / Alamy (top left), Jean Van Starten/Jupiter Images (right), ©216photo/istockphoto.com (bottom left), ©Mr Vector/stockphoto.com (background)
Illustrations by Richard Duszczak, Cartoon Studio Limited
Typeset in Stone Serif 12pt by DC Graphic Design Limited, Swanley Village, Kent.
Printed in Italy

A catalogue record for this title is available from the British Library

Author's Acknowledgements

First, I would like to thank everyone, young and old, whose company and writing I have enjoyed in creative writing workshops, in person and online, over the last 20 years.

For help with translation into languages unknown to me, I would like to thank Margery McMahon, Ira Papageorgiou, Iyad Hayatleh, Khaled Abusini, Mehui Li, I-Lin Chung and David Swinburne. I would also like to thank Steve Cook, education officer of the Royal Literary Fund which awarded me a Writing Fellowship to work with teachers in training at Glasgow University.

For their help and support within the Faculty of Education at Glasgow University, I would like to thank Professor Jim McGonigal, Dr Beth Dickson and Dr Maureen Farrell.

In addition, for help with research, I would like to thank Dr Freda Hughes (OUP), Lizzie MacGregor (librarian, the Scottish Poetry Library), Mark Burley (of Sign-a-rama, Glasgow), Lorraine Johnstone (Pollok Country Park, Glasgow), Aileen Whitelaw (Camperdown Wildlife Centre, Dundee) and Graham Lennox (Downie Farm, Aberdeen).

Thanks, too, for early advice from Karen Kerr and Eileen Galbraith, as well as Yasmin Ashby, Morag Wilson and members of the East Dunbartonshire Intervention Team.

I would also like to thank John Mitchell, Katherine Bennett and Elizabeth Hayes of Hodder Gibson for much help in putting this all together and last, but not least, Donald Beveridge, for being there, and for space and time in France in which to write this book.

Valerie Thornton

This book is dedicated to the memory of my father, Maxwell Douglas Thornton (1916–2008), whose love of words lives on…

Contents

Contents

Introduction for the Teacher

This book is designed to assist teachers delivering the Writer's Craft and Knowledge About Language elements of the National Guidelines for 5–14 English Language in Scotland. It is intended to be used with upper primary pupils at Levels C and D.

The teacher's book which accompanies this volume contains photocopiable activity sheets on which pupils can write their answers to the questions set in this pupil book.

The teacher's book also contains suggested answers to the questions in this book.

Introduction
A Short History of Language: In the Beginning...

Where Do Words Come From?

Once upon a time – long, long, ago – in a world before words and before writing, people made only movements and sounds.

Can you imagine such a time? How different would our world be without words and without writing? Think about all the things we would be unable to do...

Then, some people agreed that a particular sound should have a particular meaning. For example, that the sound "bird" would mean "a feathered creature that flies in the air".

Next, instead of drawing a bird in the sand with a stick, they agreed that the sound "bird" would be represented by the marks we know as letters, and written on dried animal skins (called parchment) with pens made from a goose feather and ink from an octopus or from soot. A thousand years ago, very few people could read or write, and books had to be handwritten, usually by monks.

Today, we know how important it is to be able to read and write, so we have schools with teachers who can help everyone to learn these skills.

When we write, we choose from the twenty-six letters of our alphabet. Our letters are made up from lines and circles, dots and curves, and arranged in different ways to record these "sounds-with-meaning" or words. We use little spaces between our words, to keep them apart. We arrange them in lines, and read them from left to right, and from the top to the bottom of the page. This language is called English.

Why Do We Have Different Languages?

If we had lived in a different country, not so far from here, we might have decided that the sound "wuz-o" would mean "bird" instead, and we would have decided to spell it "oiseau" – do you know which language this is?

"Vogel" is a word from another nearby country that also means "bird" – do you know which language this is?

Yet another word for "bird" is "ave" which is Spanish. It is pronounced "ah-vay".

Can you think of an English word that begins with "av..." that means "a place where we keep lots of wild birds"? Both this English word and the Spanish word come from another, older, language called Latin.

The Latin word for bird is "avis". Can you think of any other English words that are connected to flight or flying and that begin with "av..."? These words come from Latin too.

Why Have Some Of Our Words Come From Latin?

Latin was spoken long ago, in ancient Rome, in Italy. About 2000 years ago, when the Romans set off to conquer other countries, they brought their language with them. They conquered most of what we now call England and, around 130 AD, Emperor Hadrian built a wall, 73 miles long, right across northern England to try to keep out the fearsome Picts who lived further north.

His adopted son, Antonius Pius, pushed further north into what we now call Scotland. Around twelve years later, he built a second wall, 39 miles long, right across Scotland from the River Clyde near Glasgow, to the River Forth near Edinburgh. These walls are called Hadrian's Wall and The Antonine Wall. You can still see the remains of both walls. The Romans retreated from Britain about 50 years later, after nearly 250 years of occupation, leaving behind stones and words.

Where Else Has English Come From?

Our English language has developed not only from Latin, but from many other languages, including the Norse language which was brought to us about 1000 years ago by ancient invaders from the north called the Vikings.

Our language is always changing, with new words being added and old ones dropping away and sometimes coming back again differently.

For example, your great grandparents would have used the word "wireless" to mean "a radio". Your grandparents would have called it "a transistor radio" or just "a transistor" or "a tranny" for short. Your parents – well, ask them yourself what they call it. And the old word "wireless"? It's now coming back in the world of computing to describe mice or printers without cables.

As for the word "mouse"…!

Not Everyone Speaks and Writes English

If we had lived in a very different part of the world, our spoken and written language would have developed very differently. For example:

птица is "bird" in Russian, which uses a different alphabet from us. It is called Cyrillic after a saint named St Cyril.

πουλί is "bird" in Greek and written in the Greek alphabet.

طائر is "bird" in Arabic which is read from right to left, and from the back to the front of the book.

鳥 is "bird" in traditional Chinese. Traditional Chinese characters are read from the back to the front of the book, and from the top to the bottom of the page.

All over the world, many different languages have developed with different sounds and different ways of writing them down and reading them. Fortunately, people are usually able to learn each other's languages, so we can all communicate with each other.

However, some ways of communicating used by ancient cultures still remain a mystery today. Four hundred years ago, the Incas of South America were recording their important information and numbers by tying knots in coloured strings. They created very complex patterns with thousands of coloured knotted strings suspended from one long horizontal cord. What exactly these string "books" called "quipu" meant, remains a mystery: the Incas would have been baffled by our books too.

Letters, Words, Sentences...

Let's return from our travels and look a little more closely at how we write in English.

We have two ways of writing each letter – as a capital letter, like "B", or a small letter, like "b". Which kind of letter, capital or small, do we use most? When and why do we use the other one? (See if you can think of two reasons.)

Each letter sits on a line: some also have tails going down below the line, like "g" or "y", and some, like "d" or "f", stand up higher than the other letters.

If a letter has a tail, we call the tail a *descender*, because it descends, or goes down, below the line. If the letter stands up higher, we call the higher part an *ascender*, because it ascends, or goes up, above the line. Can you think of three other small letters with descenders? Can you think of three other small letters with ascenders? Can you think of any of our small letters that have both an ascender and a descender? (You might like to write out the alphabet before you try to answer these three questions.)

Most letters don't mean anything on their own. Can you think of any single letters that have meanings?

While words are the most important thing on the page, white spaces are also important. We've seen how we use spaces between words – becauseotherwisewewouldfinditdifficulttoreadthem – and we know that we group words into sentences which start with a capital letter and end with a full stop.

A full stop is just one of several little marks, called punctuation marks. We have dots, called full stops, to show the end of a thought or idea. Can you think of any other punctuation marks we use? See if you can think of three more. How and why do we use each of them?

If we have lots and lots of sentences, one after the other, without a break, we get confused. So we organise them into small groups called paragraphs. We take a new paragraph when something changes – a new idea, a new speaker, a new happening.

There are two ways of showing a new paragraph on the page. The first way is to start on a new line and "indent" the first line, which means that we start a little further in on the first line than we do with all the other lines. This is how new paragraphs are shown in books and newspapers and in all the stories and parts of stories in this book.

The second way, which we are using in the teaching sections of this book, is to leave a whole line blank between paragraphs. This works too and helps to make points more clearly, but it costs the publisher more to print because all the blank lines use up more paper. Indenting works well and is much cheaper in a long work like a novel or a newspaper.

If we find we have lots of paragraphs, then we group them into packages, called chapters. We take not just a new line, but a new page for each new chapter and give it a nice big heading. Then, we group our chapters together into a whole book and give it an even bigger heading, called a title, on the front cover.

Then we put all our books together, on bookshelves, in big buildings called libraries which are full of those little marks we call letters and words and which have meanings...

...and that is a brief history of language for you, which you might like to explore further on your own.

Here is a poem for you by Tom Leonard that plays with the idea of the history of language.

in the beginning

. in the beginning was the word .

in thi beginning was thi wurd

in thi beginnin was thi wurd

in thi biginnin was thi wurd

in thi biginnin wuz thi wurd

n thi biginnin wuz thi wurd

nthi biginnin wuzthi wurd

nthibiginnin wuzthiwurd

nthibiginninwuzthiwurd

. in the beginning was the sound .

Part One

Your Writing Toolkit

Vowels and Consonants

As you know, we have 26 letters in our alphabet. Our word "alphabet" comes from the Greek words for the first two letters of their alphabet – alpha (α) and beta (β).

21 of these letters are called consonants and five are called vowels. The vowels are the letters "a e i o u".

The difference between a consonant and a vowel is this: we use our lips, tongues or teeth to start off the sound of a consonant but we make vowel sounds without interrupting our breath or moving any part of our mouths. We use the smooth sound of vowels to join the rougher consonants together.

For example, if you say the word "too" and think about what your mouth is doing, you will realise your tongue clicks off the roof of your mouth to make the "t" sound, but the "oo" sound flows out smoothly after it, with your mouth still, for as long as you can breathe out.

Now try the following sounds and think about which part of your mouth is making the consonant(s) at the beginning: boo, do, moo, lee, see, she, tree, key, grey.

When we speak, we use vowels to help us express emotion. We can take longer to speak the vowels to help us get our feelings over. For example: Nooooo! Muuuum! I am soooo tired! That belongs to meeeee! Yipeeeee!

Also, when we are singing, vowels help us to stretch words and carry the tune along on them. For example, think about the way we lengthen every word when we sing the Happy Birthday song.

Sometimes the letter "y" can be used as a vowel too, sounding like "i". For example, cry, try and fly. Mostly, though, "y" is a consonant, as in yellow, you and young.

Exercise 1: Vowels and Consonants

See if you can circle the vowels in the following words. Watch for "y" and decide whether it is being used as a vowel or a consonant.

big	garden	by	metre
yard	silver	yes	window
sty	trench	hello	Mary

Nouns and Verbs

Nouns and verbs are two very important kinds of words.

Nouns are naming words, like table, coat, child, apple, water.

You can remember a noun is a naming word because *noun* and *name* both begin with the same letter "n".

Verbs are doing words, like goes, sings, eats, runs, flows.

Together, nouns and verbs make sense out of individual words.

So, for example, if we take two nouns, "Peter" and "cabbages", and there is no verb, then we do not know what the connection is between the two nouns.

We need a verb, a doing word. The verb could be any of the following: grows... eats... paints... likes... hates... throws.... Each verb creates a different relationship between Peter and cabbages.

Exercise 2: Nouns and Verbs

Can you underline the nouns in the following four sentences?

1   Jamie rides a bicycle.

2   Karen went to town.

3   The dog chased a kitten.

4   The train went to the city.

Now underline, in a different way or a different colour, the verb in each sentence.

Try reading the sentences without the verbs.

Try reading only the verbs.

We need both nouns and verbs to make sense.

Adjectives

While nouns and verbs are very important, sometimes we want to add some description. If we want to add description to a noun, we use a word called an adjective.

For example, if we say, "Jamie rides a bicycle", we know nothing about Jamie or the bicycle. Here are some adjectives:

> Big Jamie rides a tiny bicycle.
>
> Old Jamie rides a black bicycle.
>
> Young Jamie rides a new bicycle.

Can you think of any other adjectives to describe either Jamie or the bicycle?

We can have nouns without adjectives, but adjectives won't make sense without a noun. Try taking out the nouns "Jamie" and "bicycle" from the three sentences and see what happens.

Adverbs

In the same way as we use adjectives to describe nouns, so adverbs describe verbs. You can remember that an *adverb* describes a *verb* because it has the word "*verb*" in it.

So, for example, here is Jamie again.

Jamie rides his bicycle.

We know what he's doing, but we don't know exactly *how* he is doing it. Here are some adverbs which help to describe the way he is doing it.

> Jamie rides his bicycle slowly.
>
> Jamie rides his bicycle quickly.
>
> Jamie rides his bicycle stupidly.
>
> Jamie rides his bicycle carefully.

You may have noticed all these adverbs end with the letters "ly". This is a very common ending for many, but not all, adverbs. For example:

> Jamie rides his bike fast.
>
> Jamie rides his bike well.

Can you think of any other adverbs to describe the way Jamie rides his bicycle?

We will come back to the power of adjectives and adverbs to help us to create characters and to describe places later, in the section on Dialogue and Narrative (p 46). However, for now, if you think about all the different Jamies we have created with adjectives and adverbs, you will begin to see how you can create your own characters too.

Parts of Speech

We call nouns, adjectives, verbs and adverbs "parts of speech" because each one is a part of our speech and of our writing. There are other parts of speech too, which you will meet later on in your studies of English, but four are enough to begin with, here in this book.

Punctuation Marks

Capital Letters and Full Stops

Punctuation marks may be small, but they are powerful.

The word "punctuation" is connected to the word "puncture" which means "to make a hole". You or your parents may have been unlucky enough to get a puncture in a tyre, when a nail or a piece of glass makes a small hole in it and all the air escapes, causing problems for whoever was trying to travel somewhere.

In writing, punctuation marks make "holes" or gaps or pauses in what would otherwise be non-stop words.

The most important and most common punctuation mark is the full stop. This is the round dot that we put at the end of our sentences. We could use only full stops to show the ends of sentences but we also use a capital letter at the start of the first word of every sentence. Together, a capital letter and a full stop mark the beginning and end of each sentence.

A full stop followed by a capital letter is how we punctuate, or make pauses between, our sentences. The end of a sentence is where we can breathe in, before we speak again.

Exercise 3: Capital Letters and Full Stops

Here is a paragraph without the sentences marked in it. See if you can punctuate it, using only full stops and capital letters (and a red pen, if you want).

> it was another good day the sun shone in all the windows Julie knew that they would be going down to the river for a picnic she wanted to take her best pal so she phoned her the phone rang out nobody was there maybe she had already gone for a picnic without her Julie hoped not

Question Mark and Exclamation Mark

We have looked at how we use full stops at the end of sentences. We are now going to look at two other punctuation marks that we can use instead of just a full stop. They are the question mark and the exclamation mark.

Look at the next three sentences and try to explain how changing the punctuation mark at the end of each sentence changes the meaning.

> Michael's pen is on Polly's desk.
>
> Michael's pen is on Polly's desk?
>
> Michael's pen is on Polly's desk!

The first is just a simple statement telling us where the pen is. The second is asking whether Michael's pen is on Polly's desk. The third is expressing surprise that Michael's pen is on Polly's desk.

We are now going to have a closer look at question marks and exclamation marks.

Question mark

The question mark is like a full stop with a hook above it. The hook is a bit like an ear shape, perhaps listening for an answer.

We put a question mark (instead of a full stop) at the end of a sentence which is asking a question and hoping for an answer.

For example: How old are you? Where do you live? Will you help me?

Exercise 4: Question Mark or Full Stop?

Complete each of the following sentences with either a question mark or a full stop.

1 Sarah went into the garden

2 Did Lucy go too

3 Where is my T-shirt

4 You've got five pounds to spend

5 How much more do you want

6 Are you joking

7 He is late again

8 There is no bread today, is there

9 I've brought the cups

10 What time is it

Exclamation mark

The exclamation mark is like a full stop with a straight line above it. The straight line is like the stick someone might bang on the ground to emphasise the point, which is what an exclamation mark does too.

We use exclamation marks instead of just a full stop at the end of dramatic sentences or words. They indicate strong emotion and a louder way of speaking. We also use them when we are giving someone an order.

For example: No! Give me that! I hate sprouts! Stop it! Help! The bath is too hot!

Other languages use punctuation differently from English. For example, if we're writing in Spanish, we start a question with an upside-down question mark and finish it with one the right way up:

¿Cómo está usted? (How do you do?)

Similarly, in Spanish, an exclamation begins with an upside down exclamation mark and ends with one the right way up:

¡Hola! (Hello!)

Exercise 5: Full Stops, Question Marks or Exclamation Marks?

Here are 14 examples. Decide whether they work best with a full stop, a question mark or an exclamation mark.

You may find that you have a choice of punctuation marks for some of these. Complete each sentence with the mark that makes the most sense to you.

1 Go away

2 Why did you do that

3 He wanted a biscuit

4 Tell me your name right now

5 I'll write that down for you

6 Get lost

7 That dog never stops barking

8 I like spaniels and collies

9 Have you any sisters or brothers

10 I'll give you a hand

11 Your dog can't possibly be green

12 Is it a horse

13 It must be a horse

14 Horses can grow quite tall

Comma

Sometimes we write in simple sentences. A simple sentence has just one piece of information and needs only a capital letter at the beginning and a full stop at the end.

Sometimes, however, we want to write more complicated, longer sentences. This is where a comma can be useful. A comma looks like a full stop with a little tail, like a small tadpole with its head on the line and its tail below.

Commas tell us to take a little pause, inside a sentence, but not as big a pause as a full stop. They help us to make our meaning clear.

Two ways we use commas

Here are two of the main ways that we use commas: to separate items on a list and to make long sentences easier to understand. We will look at each of these ways separately.

1 Using Commas to Separate Lists of Words

Here are three sentences without commas. Read them aloud, quickly.

> I have four large green apples.
>
> We need coconut biscuits and juice.
>
> He got chocolate money and a new bike.

Without commas, the first sentence still makes sense. In the second sentence, we're not quite sure whether the writer means coconut *and* biscuits or biscuits with coconut in them. In the third sentence, we don't know whether he got chocolate *and* money or money that was made of chocolate.

Here are the same three sentences with commas this time to make the writer's meaning perfectly clear.

> I have four, large, green apples.
>
> We need coconut, biscuits and juice.
>
> He got chocolate, money and a new bike.

Exercise 6: Commas in Lists

Now try putting commas in the lists in the following seven sentences yourself. Remember that we don't put a comma before "and".

1   There were red green blue and yellow birds.

2   She saw shops houses fields and a river.

3   I need a pen a pencil a ruler and a rubber.

4   Have you got a table a chair a bed and a bookcase?

5   I ate one egg two potatoes three carrots and no peas.

6   You ate all the jelly babies two packets of crisps four chocolate biscuits and my doughnut.

7   He wore red trousers a blue shirt a baseball cap and white trainers.

Now make up three sentences of your own with correctly punctuated lists in them.

2 Using Commas in Complex Sentences

Some sentences are nice and short and simple. They only need a capital letter and a full stop. For example:

> I like dragonflies.
>
> He sat on the chair.
>
> We are going home.

Our writing would be very boring if we only used simple sentences. When we add more information to our sentences, we make them more complex. We need to use commas to keep the meaning clear. For example:

> I like dragonflies, especially green ones.
>
> Without saying a word to us, he sat on the chair.
>
> As soon as we've finished the shopping, we are going home.

Here, the main part of our sentence is separated from the extra information by a comma. Try saying these sentences aloud, putting in a pause where the commas are.

Exercise 7: One Comma in Complex Sentences

Now try putting one comma in each of the following complex sentences yourself.

1   Although he had forgotten his dinner money the dinner lady gave him a meal.
2   After I'd cleaned out the tank I put the fish back.
3   They went for a walk far further than they'd ever been before.
4   If you don't hurry up you'll get left behind.

Now look at these four sentences again and decide which of the two parts, before or after the comma, is the main part. Which part of the sentence could make sense on its own? Write down the four simple sentences.

Here are three more simple sentences.

> My uncle is late.
>
> The old lady has moved away.
>
> There are five plants on the windowsill.

Here are the same sentences made into complex sentences by adding some more information. You will notice that the extra information, because it comes in the middle of the sentence, has a comma both before and after it.

> My uncle, who is taking me to the cinema, is late.
>
> The old lady, the one with three dogs, has moved away.
>
> There are five plants, all with beautiful flowers, on the windowsill.

Exercise 8: Two Commas in Complex Sentences

Here are three complex sentences. They each need two commas. See if you can put them in the right places.

1   My paper round which I can't do next week doesn't take very long.

2   That orange butterfly you saw the one with the big circles on its wings is called a peacock butterfly.

3   Once upon a time in a faraway land there was a prince.

These are the two main uses of commas: to separate the items on a list and to make complex sentences easier to understand.

Commas are also used in the punctuation of direct speech. We will look at this in the next section.

Direct Speech or Dialogue

Direct speech or dialogue is when the actual words spoken by someone are put straight into a piece of writing. For example:

> "It's raining again," Julie said.
> Her brother, Alistair, looked up from his book.
> "That means it's a good day for reading," he replied.
> "But I want to go to the park."

We use punctuation and paragraphs to help us make it clear to our readers who is speaking and what they are saying.

Here are some guidelines to help you write direct speech correctly.

1   Take a new paragraph each time there is a new speaker, even if they say only one word.

2   Let your character speak *before* you say who is speaking. This helps your writing to flow better.

3   If you don't need to say who is speaking, then don't.

4   Put speech marks *before* the first word and *after* the last word your characters say. Speech marks are two pairs of commas which we write above the line, level with the top of the letters. The first pair of commas, which open the speech, are turned upside down, or inverted, like 66. The second two, which close the speech, are the right way up, like 99. You can remember this order because 66, which comes first, is a smaller number than 99. (Speech marks are sometimes called "inverted commas".)

5   If we are also saying who is speaking, we use a comma at the end of the sentence spoken, before we close our speech marks and before we say who is speaking. This is because the sentence isn't finished until after we have said who is speaking.

These are the main points to remember, but here are a few questions you might also like answered.

Q What if my character is asking a question or exclaiming something – where does the question mark or exclamation mark go?

 A Let's rewrite the last example a little and you can see for yourself.

> "Is it raining again?" Julie asked.
> Her brother, Alistair, looked up from his book.
> "Yes! That means it's a good day for reading!" he replied.
> "But I want to go to the park."

What would you say is the guideline for using question marks and exclamation marks within direct speech?

 Q Why is there no capital letter at "he" when Alistair replies in the third line?

 A This is because the sentence is still not finished – see guideline 5 on the previous page.

If, in the first line, we had used "she" instead of "Julie", would we have a capital letter or not at "she"? Why?

 Q Why is there a full stop after "park"?

 A This is because "park" is the end of both the speech and the sentence.

If we had added "she moaned" at the end, can you say how we would need to change the punctuation?

What if my character says more than one sentence?

 Here is another example to show you what we do.

> "It's raining again," Julie said. "I hate to see so much rain! It's rained every day for the last six months and I'm fed up with it. It's cold too."
>
> Her brother, Alistair, looked up from his book.
>
> "That means it's a good day for reading," he replied. "Why don't you go and get that book you got from Auntie Sophie for Christmas?"
>
> "But I want to go to the park."

What would you say are the guidelines for using paragraphs and speech marks, if your character says more than one sentence?

 How do I know where to put the "he said" or "she said"?

 You have choices here. You can put it in the middle of a character's speech, you can put it at the end, or you can miss it out if we already know who is speaking.

(Some writers put it at the beginning, before their characters have started to speak. This is not wrong but your writing will flow better if you let your character speak first.)

You may have noticed that we didn't say "Julie said" at the very end. That is because we already know that Julie is speaking.

We could also miss out "he replied" because we know that it is Alistair who is speaking.

Here is the passage without "he replied".

> "It's raining again," Julie said. "I hate to see so much rain! It's rained every day for the last six months and I'm fed up with it. It's cold too."
>
> Her brother, Alistair, looked up from his book.
>
> "That means it's a good day for reading. Why don't you go and get that book you got from Auntie Sophie for Christmas?"
>
> "But I want to go to the park."

Do you think the passage is better with or without "he replied"? Why?

Can you explain what has happened to the comma that we used to have at the end of the first sentence that Alistair speaks?

If we already know who is speaking, then your writing will be better if you don't keep adding "he said... she said... he said... she replied...".

Q What if my character is only thinking something and not speaking out loud?

A To avoid confusion with words that we can hear, we don't use any speech marks for thoughts, which are silent. Some publishers use italics (*like this*) to show thoughts, some don't. Next time you are reading a book where a character thinks, look closely and see what decision the publisher has made about thoughts.

Finally, if you want an excellent example of how to use direct speech, look at the way Evelyn Jean-Louis uses it in "Fahim 911" (p 189). Look carefully at her use of paragraphs, at her use of speech marks, at how she weaves speech and story-telling together, and at how she isn't always saying "he said" or "she said".

Different Kinds of Writing

We have many different reasons for writing. Here are four different kinds of writing that you might like to use.

1 Personal writing

This is when we write as ourselves, about things that are important to us, or that have happened to us. If you write your life story, or a diary, or about where you went on your holiday, or about how you feel about fox-hunting or wind farms, this is all personal writing. It lets the reader get to know you as a person.

2 Imaginative Writing

This is when we make things up, or when we mix reality with fiction. We use our imaginations to ask questions like, "What if...?" What if I met a monster on my way to school? What if I had a brother in America? What if there were no more cars? What if I could fly?

Imaginative writing often starts with something real and then moves off into our imaginations. It can be close to us, like pretending we have a pet, or a brother or sister, different from our real ones. Or it can take off and take us miles and years away from our present reality into space, or into the distant past or far into the future. Our imaginations are powerful tools for helping us to come up with ideas no one has already thought of.

We use *personal* writing to remember events or people that are important to us, or to help us work out how we think or feel about something.

We use *imaginative* writing to have fun, to entertain ourselves and others, with scary, surprising or funny stories.

3 Functional Writing

This is writing that is, first and foremost, useful. The following are examples of functional writing: instructions for assembling a

PC, a recipe for lentil broth, a newspaper article about a plane crash or a sporting event.

Functional writing often contains facts and interesting information. Its purpose is to let you know about something, rather than to entertain you. Very often, writers of functional writing are much less well-known than writers of fiction or poetry. This is because the information is more important than the writer of it.

4 Environmental Writing

This is where you find the biggest size of letters and the fewest number of words.

Environmental writing is all the words you see outside in the world. Environmental writing includes signs on the streets and in public places like shops, cinemas and museums. It is usually instructions that people must obey (Keep Clear, No Stopping, This Way, Exit, No Entry, Private), or information that people might need (Cedar Avenue, Hardware Store, Tourist Information, Roadworks Ahead), or advertising some company or product (Buy One Get One Free, More Bargains Inside).

Can you think of any environmental writing in your classroom or school? Have a look around you on your way home today and see how many words you can read in your environment. Look for words on shops or streets, and also words moving past you on lorries, vans and buses. Can you imagine how different our life would become without environmental writing?

Different Kinds of Writers

Just as we have different kinds of writing, so we have different kinds of writers. Each writer writes one letter at a time, and gradually builds up their work into a final form.

Authors are writers who write imaginative books and novels or short stories. Authors also write personally about things that they have done, like climbing Mount Everest or being a film star. Authors use letters, words, sentences, paragraphs, chapters and then give their books titles.

Poets are writers who write poems. Poets use letters, words, sentences and titles. Instead of paragraphs and chapters, they write verses. You can usually tell by the way the words look on a page whether it is a story or a poem. For example, look at pp 98, 107, 117 and 159 and see if you can tell by the way each page looks whether it is a story or a poem.

Journalists are writers who write for newspapers and magazines. Journalists use letters, words, sentences, paragraphs and then give their articles headlines, not titles.

Sign-writers create environmental writing. They are not writers, but artists who choose to work with big letters and logos. They design the shape and colour of the letters and the background so that their signs are clear and eye-catching.

In the old days, before computers, sign-writers were skilled with brushes and paint because all the lettering was done by hand. Now, they are skilled operators of computer design packages. Sign-writers use only letters and words (and logos): they never use chapters or titles. Why do you think they don't need chapters or titles?

Two Very Useful Books for Writers: Dictionary and Thesaurus

Dictionary

The word "dictionary" comes to us from the Latin verb meaning to speak: *dicere*.

Dictionaries are books that are filled with long lists of the words we speak, arranged in alphabetical order. They explain the meaning of each word and the way we should use them. Dictionaries can help us to pronounce words too.

Some dictionaries also tell us which older language, or other language, the word has come from. These dictionaries are called etymological dictionaries.

Dictionaries use codes to explain things. If they didn't, they would be too long and too heavy. Dictionaries also tell you what part of speech a word is, using "n" for noun, "v" for a verb, "adj" for adjective and "adv" for adverb.

Here is a dictionary entry for you from the ninth edition of *The Chambers Dictionary* (2003):

> Greyhound... /grā'hownd / *n* a tall, slender dog of an ancient breed bred for their great speed and keen sight. [OE *grīghiund* (cf ON *greyhundr*, or *grey*)]

This tells us [1] the word, [2] how to pronounce it, [3] that it is a noun, [4] what it means, [5] that the word comes to us from Old English (OE) and [6] that this can be compared (cf) to the [7] Old Norse (ON).

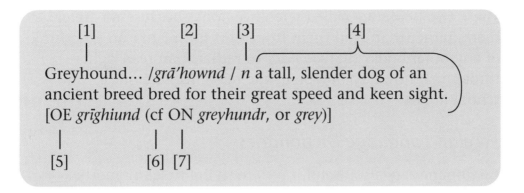

```
     [1]           [2]    [3]           [4]
      |             |      |      ⌐‾‾‾‾‾‾‾‾‾‾‾⌐
Greyhound... /grā'hownd / n a tall, slender dog of an
ancient breed bred for their great speed and keen sight.
[OE grīghiund (cf ON greyhundr, or grey)]
      |             |  |
     [5]          [6] [7]
```

Thesaurus

A thesaurus is another book that will help you to become a better writer. The word "thesaurus" is a Latin word which comes from a very similar Greek word "thésauros" which means a place where knowledge is stored.

Instead of explaining the meaning of the word, which is what a dictionary does, a thesaurus lists other words with similar meanings. So if you are writing about colours, and you don't want to keep using the word yellow, a thesaurus can offer you lots more words connected to yellow in some way. There are often words you will never have heard of, and that you may never use, but there will also be some that could be helpful.

Here is what you can find if you look up the adjective "yellow" in Roget's *Thesaurus* (1979):

Yellow, gold, golden, aureate, gilt, gilded; fulvous, fallow, sallow, honey-pale; yellowish, bilious, jaundiced, xanthic; luteous; sandy, flaxen, fair-haired, blond, platinum blond; creamy, cream-coloured; citrine, lemon-coloured, straw-coloured, butter-coloured.

The best thing about a dictionary or a thesaurus is that each is full of new thoughts and ideas. We find ourselves side-tracked by other words: sometimes we even forget what word we were looking up in the first place. We can find unexpected connections and new ideas can develop.

These two books are called reference books because we "refer" to them, rather than read them from start to finish. Can you think of any other books that we refer to rather than read right through? If not, have a look in the reference section of your school library.

Foreign Language Dictionaries

Dictionaries are also useful if we are trying to learn another language. For example, if we have a French dictionary, it helps us to translate between French and English.

The first half of a French dictionary has words in French, arranged in alphabetical order, each followed by their meaning in English. So if we find a French word we don't understand, for example, "libellule", we can look this up in the French part and it will tell us this means "dragonfly".

Or, if we want to know what the French word for carpet is, we look up "carpet" in the English part of the book and we learn that the French word is "tapis". This word is connected to our English word "tapestry". Can you think of any link between tapestries and carpets?

Rhythm

Seeing and Hearing Rhythm

Our lives are full of rhythm. The rhythm of our heartbeat is:

da-DUM... da-DUM... da-DUM...

Our breathing goes:

in... out... in... out...

When we walk our feet go:

step – step – step –

When we run, our feet (and perhaps our hearts too) go:

thump-thump-thump

When we sleep: zzzzz...zzzzz...zzzzz...

These are all rhythms. Rhythm is a pattern of sound or movement. It involves repetition – one heartbeat or one step doesn't make a rhythm. It also involves time – rhythm can be fast or slow or a pattern of both.

Rhythm also involves stress, or emphasis, where some sounds are louder and some are quieter. If you imagine someone using a hammer to drive in a nail, you can both see and hear the rhythm. The stress is when the hammer hits the nail – we hear a very short loud noise – then there are a few seconds of quiet until the next hit:

HIT silence HIT silence HIT silence

How would this rhythm change if the person hit their thumb instead?

Can you think of any more examples of rhythm around you that you can see or hear?

Rhythm and Music

Do you remember learning to clap your hands to a song, or to dance in time to the music? Rhythm and music are closely connected.

Rhythm, in language, is also like a kind of music. We find it more in poetry, which is closer to song than stories are.

To understand how rhythm works, we need to become aware of how words in English have stressed and unstressed syllables. For example, if we take the word "continue", which has three syllables, we don't say it evenly, as a Dalek would. We put stress on the middle syllable, making it longer and louder than the other two, which are unstressed.

ᵕ / ᵕ
con-**tin**-ue

Every word in English can be marked with these symbols (ᵕ and /) to show the stressed and unstressed syllables.

For example:

ᵕ / ᵕ / ᵕ
con-**tin**-u-**a**-tion – this has five syllables, two stressed and three unstressed.

Exercise 9: Stress Patterns

Can you mark the stress patterns on the following words? Listen very carefully to the way you say each word. Exaggerate the stresses to make it easier for you to hear them.

happy

Monday

under

Wednesday

September

hurricane

Aberdeen

understand

wonderful

magnificent

good

Here is a very rhythmic poem or song that you will probably already know. Read it aloud. You will be able to feel the rhythm without actually knowing what is happening.

> Humpty Dumpty sat on a wall
> Humpty Dumpty had a great fall
> All the King's horses and all the King's men
> Couldn't put Humpty together again.

When we mark in the pattern of stresses, you can see why it has such a strong rhythm.

   /   ˇ   / ˇ / ˇ ˇ /

Humpty **Dump**ty **sat** on a **wall**

    /   ˇ   / ˇ / ˇ ˇ   /

Humpty **Dump**ty **had** a great **fall**

/   ˇ   ˇ   / ˇ ˇ / ˇ   ˇ   /

All the King's **hors**es and **all** the King's **men**

    /   ˇ ˇ   /   ˇ ˇ / ˇ ˇ /

Couldn't put **Hump**ty to**ge**ther a**gain**.

The stressed syllables are the ones that carry the rhythm. How many do we have in each line? What do you notice about the start and finish of each line?

If we had any more stresses, it would break the pattern. Try adding the word "Dumpty" to the last line, read the poem again, and you'll see and feel what happens.

Many poems for younger children have a very strong rhythm. This makes them easier to remember and it is also good fun to learn them and to chant or sing them together.

You can see Edwin Morgan using different rhythms in some parts of his poem, "Red Deer" (p 98). For example, read the next two lines aloud and listen to the rhythm:

Who could cull us, who could kill us,
smell of stalkers couldn't chill us.

If we mark in the stresses, you will see a bold, strong pattern, like the bold, strong deer:

/ ˘ / ˘ / ˘ / ˘
Who could **cull** us, **who** could **kill** us,

/ ˘ / ˘ / ˘ / ˘
smell of **stalk**ers **couldn't chill** us.

Exercise 10: More Stress Patterns

Another use of rhythm, creating a different feeling in the same poem is:

> soon comes snow
> when you must go
> starving and gaunt
> downhill to haunt
> the homes of men.
> What then, what then?

Can you mark in the stresses and say what kind of feeling the words and the rhythm make now?

By now, you should understand a little about how rhythm works in our English language. As a writer, you can use it in your own poems too.

Rhyme

Like rhythm, rhyme is found mostly in songs and poems. When a writer uses rhyme, the sound of the word is as important as its meaning.

Rhyme is created when two or more words have the same sound at the end of them. For example, the following words rhyme:

me, see, flee, be

wing, sing, fling, bring

cook, book, look, duke

fly, try, by, sigh

You will notice that words can rhyme without being spelt in exactly the same way: rhyme is about sound not spelling.

Can you think of any words that rhyme with bat, or with sun, or with house, or with fur?

Rhyme is often found at the ends of lines in poems or songs. Writers can have fun making different patterns with the order of the rhymes.

In the previous section, we looked at "Humpty Dumpty" from the point of view of its rhythm. Let's look at it now from the point of view of its rhyme. We can work out the rhyming scheme (or pattern) by using the letters of the alphabet, like this:

Humpty Dumpty sat on a wall	a
Humpty Dumpty had a great fall	a ("all" sound)
All the King's horses and all the King's men	b
Couldn't put Humpty together again.	b ("en" sound)

So, the rhyming scheme for "Humpty Dumpty" is aabb. You will notice the last two rhyming words, men/again, are not spelt the same way but the *sound* is still the same.

We call the first rhyme sound "a". Then, each time we find a new rhyme, we use the next letter of the alphabet for it.

Here is another rhyming scheme:

Mary had a little lamb	a
Its fleece was white as snow	b
And everywhere that Mary went	c
The lamb was sure to go.	b

Here, the writer has rhymed only the second and fourth lines, using an abcb rhyming scheme.

Exercise 11: Rhyming Schemes

Can you mark in the rhyming scheme for the following three poems? Remember, each time you find a new rhyme, you use the next letter of the alphabet for it. (Start with the letter "a" for each poem.)

Twinkle, twinkle, little star
How I wonder what you are.
Up above the world so high,
Like a diamond in the sky,
Twinkle, twinkle, little star
How I wonder what you are.

One, two,
Buckle my shoe.
Three, four,
Knock at the door.
Five, six,
Pick up sticks.
Seven, eight,
Lay them straight.

Little Miss Muffet
Sat on a tuffet
Eating her curds and whey
Along came a spider
And sat down beside her
And frightened Miss Muffet away.

Now have a look at Edwin Morgan's poem, "Clydesdale" (p 152), and work out the rhyming scheme he has used. Surprising, isn't it?

This is a poem with a very strong pattern of rhythm and rhyme. Edwin has had a lot of fun playing with sound and meaning and arranging the words on the page.

You can have fun learning to use rhythm and rhyme yourself, if you turn to the section on limericks (p 127).

Now have a look at Ted Hughes' poem, "Moon-Ravens" (p 183). Can you work out the rhyming scheme here? You will notice some of the rhyme sounds are close, but not exactly the same sound. This is called *half-rhyme*. Here, the consonant sounds stay the same but the vowel sounds change a little. For example: kill/cull, bat/bet, salt/silt. Poets do this to make their rhymes less obvious, so that they are less in-your-face than full rhymes. They also do this so that the meaning doesn't get lost behind very obvious rhymes.

Point of View

Each and every one of us sees the world from our own unique point of view, from inside only our own heads and through only our own eyes.

However, it helps us to understand and get on with other people if we try to see things from their point of view as well, as if we were inside their heads, looking out through their eyes.

For example, if your friend, Lisa, is supposed to come for tea and arrives an hour late, you might be angry with her for not letting you know. You are seeing the situation from only your point of view.

However, if Lisa explains that her little brother broke his arm that afternoon and that she's been waiting with him and their mum for hours in casualty, then you can begin to see things from her point of view. You can understand how worrying, and perhaps boring, it must have been. Instead of being angry with her for keeping you waiting, you feel sorry for her and realise how hungry she must be.

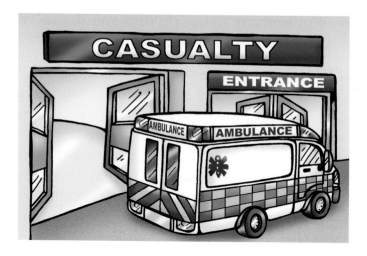

This is what we mean by seeing things from a different point of view.

Writers often decide to use a different point of view to make their writing more interesting.

For example, Anne Donovan, who is a grown-up woman, has written her story, "Tigger" (p 106), as if she were an 11-year-old boy called Joe, who has to decide whether or not to give away his beloved pet cat. She has written this story from Joe's point of view.

Look at the first two paragraphs of the story and you will see how well Anne has used this point of view.

Another writer, Maureen Sullivan, has also used a different point of view in her story "An Eye for an Eye" (p 171). Look at the opening of this story and decide from whose point of view Maureen is telling it.

Look also at "Fahim 911", by Evelyn Jean-Louis (p 189). From whose point of view has Evelyn chosen to tell this story?

Why do you think these three writers have chosen to write their stories from these points of view? How well do you think these stories would have worked if they had been told from the writer's own point of view as an adult?

You too can choose to tell a story from a different point of view. You can pretend to be older, or younger, or that you live in a different time, or a different country, or that you are a boy instead of a girl, or the other way round.

Characterisation: Creating Characters

Characters are the people or creatures we make up to put into our writing. All of the characters in Parts Two and Three of this book are made up, but they are made up so well that when we read the stories or poems we can think they are real.

So, how do we create characters?

If we write about someone we know, then we are writing about a real person. If we take an interesting little bit of one person we know, and an unusual little bit of someone else, and add a few more carefully chosen details, then instead of just describing someone we know, we are creating our own character.

 ## Exercise 12: Creating Characters

We can create a character by asking and answering the following questions. When you answer them, try to think of unusual answers, probably not the first answer you think of. The more questions you ask and the more answers you create, the more real your character becomes.

Looks

What does my character look like?

Their hair? Their face – ugly, pretty? Their eyes – kind or unkind, colour? Are they fat or thin? Tall or small? Their hands – nails bitten or long? Their clothes – fashionable, dirty, worn? Are there any other details of their appearance that you can think of?

Sounds

What does my character sound like?

Their voice – quiet, loud, soft, harsh? Do they have a lisp or stammer? Do they speak slowly or quickly? Do they make other noises – sniffing, coughing, giggling, clicking their knuckles? Are there any other sounds that you can think of?

Smells

What does my character smell of?

Shampoo? Chip fat? Fabric conditioner? Perfume? Unwashed? Sweaty? Something else?

Other Questions

What is my character's name?

What age is my character?

Where does my character live?

How does my character move?

What does my character love?

What does my character hate?

What does my character most want?

What is stopping my character getting this?

If you answer all of these questions, you will have created a solid character. You will know enough about this character for them to star as a main character in a story of yours. You can create another, entirely different, main character by answering the same questions but with very different answers.

Main Characters and Minor Characters

The main character is the most important character in any piece of writing. Sometimes there are several main characters. For example, in "The Stag" (p 89), there are two main characters: Joe and the narrator who is telling the story. There are also other characters who are less important to the story than the two children. We call less important characters "minor characters".

Exercise 13: Main and Minor Characters

Here are six other characters from "The Stag": Mum, the stag, a crowd, two policemen, Miss Cleckton, some men. Can you place each of them into one of the two groups below, either main characters or minor characters? Think about how important they are to the story and about how well you feel you know them.

Main Characters   **Minor Characters**

Joe

the narrator

In "Tigger" (p 106), Anne Donovan has created the following characters: Tigger, Mum, Dad, Danny and Joe (who is the narrator). Can you place them in order of importance to the story and try to say how many of them are main characters and how many are minor characters?

There are no correct answers to these questions, but thinking about possible answers will help you to realise that not all characters in stories are equally important.

In most of the writing you do, whether stories or poems, you will need main and minor characters.

You will also find well-drawn main characters in "All That Glitters" (p 158), "An Eye for an Eye" (p 171) and "A Symbol of Hope" (p 197).

These three stories, along with "The Stag" and "Tigger", are all stories that are based on relationships between characters where feelings are important. Can you say what are the important relationships and feelings in any or all of these five stories?

In the science fiction story "Zoo" (p 135), we still have main characters, but the emphasis is more on the strangeness of what is happening, on the fantastic setting and creatures, than on the feelings of Professor Hugo. This is a story based more on action than on character: where *what* happens in the story is more important than the character *to whom* it happens.

You can also find characters in poems. "Age Concern" (p 82) has two very different characters and although we don't learn much about them, we do learn how they relate to each other. In "Island School" (p 143), we also have characters: George Mackay Brown creates them by describing sounds and smells and movements.

Motivation

The first stage in writing a story is to create characters but, now that we have created our characters, how do we get them to act?

This is where motivation comes in. If you are motivated, then you have a strong reason for wanting to do something, or get something, or change something, or keep something the same. Hunger motivates you to go and look for food. Lack of money motivates you to take on a paper round. Wanting to get good marks motivates you to do homework.

Earlier, we answered questions in order to create characters. Here are the last four questions again:

What does my character love?

What does my character hate?

What does my character most want?

What is stopping my character getting this?

The answers to these questions help you to work out what motivates your character, what drives them, what makes them tick. It might be their desire to become an Olympic diving champion, or to stop their noisy neighbours keeping them awake at night, or to learn to use sign language.

Conflict

Conflict is what happens when one person wants something and someone else wants the opposite. Conflict is when two people are motivated in opposite directions. For example, if you *really* want to watch television and your mum *really* wants you to do your homework, then there is conflict between you and your mum. If you want your bedroom painted green and your dad wants to paint it white, then there is conflict between you and your dad. On a bigger scale, if two countries are in extreme conflict with each other, we call that a war.

Plot and Narrative

If someone asks you "What happened in the film last night?" and you reply "First this… then this… then this… and at the end…", then you are telling your friend what the *plot* was. The plot is the chain of events that happens in a piece of imaginative writing, whether it is on the page, on a screen or on the stage.

We can create a plot by creating characters who are in some kind of conflict with each other which makes things happen. Our story, which is also called a *narrative*, explores this conflict. ("Narrative" is a slightly more technical word for "story" that we use when we are looking closely at how stories work.)

An example of how we can create a plot from conflict can be seen in "Tigger" (p 106). Here, the conflict is caused by Danny's allergy to his brother's cat. If there were no allergy, everything would be fine and there would be no story to tell, no narrative.

But, instead, Anne Donovan has created conflict. The biggest conflict is inside Joe: he is torn between losing Tigger and helping Danny. Conflict doesn't always have to be *between* people, it can be inside one person too.

There are other conflicts in "Tigger" too. Joe's mum is also quietly in conflict with him because she wants him to decide to let Tigger go and she knows he doesn't want to. Danny is in conflict with his asthma and eczema which make him suffer. There is also a hint that Joe is in conflict with Danny, jealous of him for coming between him and his mum and their teas out together in the café. So, when we look at this story this way, we can see that there is a lot of conflict driving this narrative.

Another example of conflict driving the narrative can be found in "The Stag" (p 89). Here, the conflict is direct and violent: the stag fights its own reflection in a shop window. The way the two children feel about the stag makes this into a sad story.

Behind this story, and behind Edwin Morgan's poem, "Red Deer" (p 98), is a bigger conflict: deer are not at peace with their environment because there are too many deer for the land to support.

Can you say what conflict is in, and behind, "Fahim 911" (p 189) and "A Symbol of Hope" (p 197)?

The important thing to remember when you are trying to create characters and a narrative is that if everything is nice and happy you will have no story. Something has to go wrong, conflict has to develop inside, or between, your characters. If Joe hated Tigger, there would be no story. If the stag ran back into the hills, there would be no story. We need problems, difficult choices, obstacles or challenges before a story can happen. This is why the last four questions for creating characters are so important.

Dialogue and Narrative

Earlier (p 22), we looked at how to punctuate direct speech, using speech marks and commas.

Now that we know how to lay it out, let's look at how we can use the words we put into our characters' mouths not only to create our characters but also to tell the story, or drive the narrative.

Here are two characters speaking to each other:

> "Hello."
> "Hello."
> "How are you?"
> "Fine. How are you?"
> "OK."

We don't learn very much at all from this exchange, apart from that there are two people, both friendly and both well. There is little information and no conflict.

Here are another two characters speaking to each other:

> "Hello, Jimmy!"
> "Crikey, Steph, you gave me such a fright!"
> "So where is it, then? Or do I have to make you tell me?"
> "Please! No! Put that away!"
> "Ten million pounds, Jimmy… you going to tell me or not?"
> "OK, OK, just please don't shoot me!"

Now, using only dialogue and conflict, we have a much clearer picture of two men: one has a gun and is very angry, the other is terrified. We also learn that ten million pounds is involved, that Jimmy knows where the money is and that Steph wants it.

The dialogue is both creating the characters of Jimmy and Steph, and moving the plot along.

We can improve this scene by adding some description to the narrative, using adjectives (p 12) and adverbs (p 13) to help us.

> Jimmy sat down, sighing loudly, in the Cosy Rose Café. He lifted a steaming mug of hot chocolate to his lips. The smell reminded him of his childhood, long ago, when his life had been simpler.
> "Hello, Jimmy!"
> The sneering edge to the voice behind him made Jimmy's blood run cold. He clattered his mug down onto the table, untasted, and turned round.
> "Crikey, Steph, you gave me such a fright! Want a hot chocolate, mate?" he said, trying to keep his voice steady.

"So where is it, then? Or do I have to make you tell me?"

Slowly Steph reached inside his black leather jacket and Jimmy saw the ugly glint of metal.

"Please! No! Put that away!"

"Ten million pounds, Jimmy… you going to tell me or not?"

Steph slid into the seat opposite Jimmy in a cloud of cheap aftershave and snapped his fingers at the bored waitress who was polishing her perfect nails at the sticky bun counter.

"OK, OK, just please don't shoot me!"

You should now be able to see how this fragment is beginning to come to life: how the dialogue and details of smell, sound and place, and the use of adjectives and adverbs, all help to create people, places and feelings.

You can do this yourself, by asking what each sentence you write is adding to your story. Is it adding to the characterisation, or to the plot, or to the description of the setting? Setting is what we are going to have a closer look at in the next section.

Setting the Scene

Making up stories involves asking and answering questions.

The most useful questions are:

Who? What? Where? Why? When? How? What if?

When we create characters, we answer the Who? question.

When we create plot and narrative, we answer the What? Why? When? How? and What if? questions.

Where? is the question that will help us create the setting.

As readers, we usually like to have some idea of where a story or poem is set. We don't need to know every precise detail, if the setting is in the background. So, for example, all we know in the earlier café fragment is that it is called the Cosy Rose Café, that it sells sticky buns and hot chocolate and that the waitress is bored. We can imagine the rest ourselves. What else can you imagine as part of this setting? What might the tables be like? The floor? Anything on the walls? The lighting? The temperature? The view from the windows?

If, however, the place itself is important, then we will find much more detailed description of it. If you look at "Island School" (p 143) or "A Symbol of Hope" (p 197) you will see that both writers use their senses of hearing and smell to give us a strong idea of what their very different settings are like.

Description

How can we write good description?

Let's take a garden. Even the words "a garden" should be giving you some idea, but a good writer will give their readers more details.

> There was grass in the middle and flower beds with brightly coloured flowers round the edges.

This gives us a better picture but the description could still be improved. If we describe the flowers as "brightly coloured" we are being lazy and making the reader work to imagine the actual colours.

If you stop and think and see the place in your mind's eye before you start writing, it can help you to create good description. Try to hear it and smell it too. In the same way as we can create characters by using little bits of several real people, so we can create our setting by using little bits of real places to help us.

As with characters, if your place is nice and ordinary, it won't have the same power as somewhere more unusual. Here is another description of the garden.

> There was a neatly cut, moss-free, daisy-free lawn in the centre of the garden. Around this perfect, green square were flowerbeds with pink and white roses, orange marigolds and big, blue bell-flowers that were nodding gently in the warm breeze. The scent of roses drifted over the grass and the air was buzzing with the sound of bees busy gathering pollen from the flowers.

This is better, but quite normal description. We need to add something more unusual, more in conflict with the neat and tidy flower beds and grass. We could add dozens of large gnomes, or a bull that has escaped from the field next door, or a piano... or a person.

In the next section, we are going to see how to connect characters to the setting.

Connecting Characters to the Setting

Setting always works better when you connect your characters to it. The garden in the previous section is not connected to anyone – yet. Let's add Bridget.

Bridget wrinkled her nose as the smell of manure from the farm next door drifted over her beautiful garden. She could see a small herd of black bullocks circling in the distance. She had planted another twenty roses this spring to try to hide the smell.

"Dreadful today, isn't it, Mr Tobias?" she said, addressing the largest of a group of gnomes with red caps, white beards and blue jackets that lined the gravel path next to her perfect lawn.

Suddenly, she heard a loud bellowing. The bullocks in the field were now swirling around in a large dangerous-looking black mass. They lowered their heads and began charging towards her. Bridget took one look at her delicate wooden fence, grabbed Mr Tobias by his pointed ears, hauled him out of the ground and stood there, holding Mr Tobias as a shield in front of her.

Here, the setting is connected to the narrative and to the character. If some of the items in the setting are important to the narrative, then it is easy for you to connect the two together. For example, instead of saying that there are gnomes in the garden, we make Bridget speak to one and then pull it out of the ground.

Instead of saying there is a farm next door, we make the smell of the farm annoy Bridget.

Here is an example from "A Symbol of Hope" (p 199) where the character and place are connected together very well.

> In front of him was a large barren field covered in a sticky black slime. Here and there, stick-like objects, which he knew at one time must have been plants, stuck out of the ground.

If John hadn't connected his character, Michael, to the place, it would read:

> There was a large barren field covered in a sticky black slime. Here and there, stick-like objects stuck out of the ground.

So, when you are describing the setting, try to connect your characters to it and it will be better. Take time to see, hear and feel the place in your head and it will be much easier for you.

Using Setting to Create Atmosphere

If you include the weather, the time of day, colours and sounds, these can all help you to create an atmosphere in your writing.

If you want to create a feeling of sadness, what kind of weather would you choose? And what time of day? Are there any colours or smells that you can associate with sadness?

If you wanted to create a feeling of happiness, what weather would you choose? Which colours, smells and sounds can you associate with happiness?

If you want to create a scary atmosphere, what time of day and what kind of weather would you choose?

If we wanted to use the weather to create a sense of threat or anger in the fragment about Bridget, we could add heavy black clouds and a clammy feel to the air, the kind of atmosphere we experience just before a thunderstorm breaks.

Planning and Structuring Your Story

Many of the skills we have looked at so far belong to the preparation stages.

Before we start writing, we need to create unusual characters with a problem, we need to decide our setting, and how to fit our characters into it. We also need to think about what conflict we can create to give us a plot and we need to decide what is going to change between the start and the end of our story.

Some writers do this in their heads, others prefer to make notes – lots of notes. Some writers just start writing and see where the story takes them. If you are not used to doing this, it can lead to a dead end, when you run out of ideas halfway through. It is better to brainstorm lots of ideas before you begin writing and then you have a better chance of getting to the end.

Openings

The first sentence of any story is very important. It is what draws the reader into your story by making them curious.

Here are three first sentences from stories in this book.

> It was all the angel's fault.
>
> He wis a legend, so he wis: well, at least in our livin room.
>
> My hands were slippery.

These openings work because they are surprising. We want to know how the angel can be to blame for something, we want to know who was a living-room legend and we want to know whose hands were slippery and why.

These openings work because they give us *some* information but keep other details back, which are then revealed later on in the story.

Look back at some of the first sentences of stories that you have already written. Could you have made them better? Always try to start your stories with openings that make your readers curious.

Titles

It is usually easy to come up with a title which is like a label. Sometimes a label title is a good idea. Some of the titles in Part Three of this book are labels, like "The Stag" or "Red Deer" or "Island School". These titles tell you what the piece of writing is about.

Other titles are more intriguing, like "All That Glitters", "Fahim 911" or "A Symbol of Hope".

You can choose whether you want a label title or an intriguing title. Your title should be connected to your story or poem in some way, but it shouldn't give away the ending.

Your best title probably won't be the first title you think of. Some writers can take ages to find the right title.

Drafting and Redrafting

Writers almost never produce their best writing without editing and redrafting their work.

This means that they go over and over a piece of writing, changing a word here or there, changing it back again, rewriting a section, adding some details, moving paragraphs or verses around, changing the beginning, changing the ending and making yet another cup of coffee.

Your writing will improve if you not only take time to plan it properly, but if you also take time to redraft it. You can get useful feedback on your work from a writing buddy who can see your writing from a reader's point of view. They, and you, can use the following ten questions to work out whether you can improve your writing.

Checklist of ten questions for your first draft

1 Have I got a good title?

2 Have I got a good opening?

3 Have I got any unusual characters?

4 Have I described the setting?

5 Have I connected my characters to the setting?

6 Have I used weather or time of day to create atmosphere?

7 Have I got any conflict?

8 Have I got any action?

9 Has something changed by the end?

10 Have I used any dialogue?

If you have answered "yes" to all ten questions, well done!

If not, see whether you could improve your story now…

Part Two

The Writer's Craft Task

Note: you will notice that some of the words here are printed in **red** followed by a page number. If you do not understand any of these words, please turn to this page where you will find the term explained.

The Writer's Craft Task is good fun. It lets you "put on the hat" of another writer and makes imaginative writing easier for you because the story is already started.

To do this task well, you need two skills. First, the skill to work out what the writer is doing and, second, the skill to do it yourself. In the following pages, we will develop both of these skills.

Chapter 1

Practice Text
A Good Night Out

Here is the start of a story that we can work through together.

Read the story twice before looking at the questions that follow.

Mrs Todd belongs to the world that begins when our day ends. She passes the daylight hours sleeping with her two young cubs in a shady den in the bushes, down by the river that runs through the park. All around them, the city hums and buzzes like a busy hive while they doze, nose to tail, waiting for the world to quieten and darken.

As soon as dusk falls and the city settles down, Mrs Todd stretches her paws and her long spine and gives herself a shake from the black tip of her nose, to the white point at the end of her long ginger tail. Tonight, she is going to show her cubs the world beyond their den.

"Wake up, Mogs!" she says quietly to her male cub, nudging him with a paw.

She noses Pixie, her young vixen, to waken her.

"Come on, Pixie! We're going out into the world tonight."

"You mean we get to come too, instead of waiting forever for you to come back with food?" Pixie says, her eyes wide at the thought.

"You're going to learn to find your own food, tonight!"

"Great!" she chirps. "What do we have to do? I'm starving!"

"Keep very quiet and follow me, and do exactly as I say!"

Slowly, carefully, Mrs Todd leads her two cubs up the bank and through the deserted park. The moon slides out from behind a cloud and turns the world silver. The scents of the earth and plants tickle the noses of the young cubs, who want to stop and investigate everything. Mogs is trailing behind, full of curiosity about this new world.

"Hey! What's this?" he calls, patting a pine cone with his paw. It rolls away rustling and he pounces on it.

"Leave it! You can't eat that. You can play with it on the way back," Mrs Todd says, "but we must find food first. Now stay close to me, like I told you!"

They reach the closed iron gates of the park and squeeze below the bottom rail.

"Wow!" Pixie says, looking wide-eyed for the first time at a road and cars and high tenements with lights at the windows.

"This way, quick!" Mrs Todd says, sidling up the cobbled bin lane, away from the bright orange of the street lights.

Ahead of them are long rows of silvery bins, stuffed to overflowing with black rubbish bags. There are more rubbish bags dumped on the ground.

"Now, what do you think we can find for dinner tonight?"

Here are some questions, with answers, to help you become aware of what the writer is doing.

Fourteen Questions to Help You

1 What is this piece of writing about, that is, what is the subject of it? Maybe the title gives you a clue?

   Subject – a vixen takes her cubs out of their den for the first time to teach them how to find food.

2 Why has the writer written it, that is, what is their purpose? To entertain you? To give you a particular feeling? To inform you? Something else?

   Purpose – to entertain, and perhaps to teach us about how foxes can survive in cities.

3 Who is this story written for, that is, who do you feel is the audience for this story?

   Audience – young children who like stories where animals can talk like people.

4 What kind of writing is it? Is it **imaginative writing**? (p 27) Is it **personal writing**? (p 27) Is it **functional writing**? (p 27) Can you say how you know this?

   Imaginative writing, because foxes can't talk.

5 Does the writer use many **adjectives** (p 12) or **adverbs** (p 13)? Can you give two examples, from the passage, of an adjective and two of an adverb?

   Adjectives – quite a few e.g."shady" (den) and "long" (spine).

   Adverbs – a few e.g. (she says) "quietly" and "slowly, carefully" (Mrs Todd leads…)

6 Can you see any **question marks** (p 15) or **exclamation marks** (p 16)? Why is the writer using them?

   Question marks – because the cubs want to know lots of things, and at the end, the mother wants them to work out how to find food themselves.

➔

Fourteen Questions to Help You continued

Exclamation marks – the cubs are excited and are exclaiming in wonder and surprise.

7 Does the writer use long, medium or short sentences or a mixture of all three? Do you see any *very* short sentences with only three or four words?

A mixture of lengths including, in the dialogue, some very short sentences.

8 Do you see any patterns or repetitions in the writing? Why do you think the writer has done this?

Maybe "slowly, carefully..." to emphasise the care and slowness? "doze, nose" – rhyme

9 Is the writer telling the story as if it has happened to them, using "I"? Or, is the writer narrating the story as if it has happened to someone else, using "he" or "she"?

Using "he" and "she".

10 Is the writer using any **direct speech** (p 22)?

Yes.

11 Can you see any **similes** (p 92)? Can you quote one or two?

Yes: "like a busy hive".

12 Has the writer **set the scene** (p 49) by describing the place where the story is happening? You are going to continue the story so can you think of anything that you could add to describe this place?

Yes – the park at night, and the city streets and the bin lane with lots of rubbish bags.

➔

We could add details about the stuff in the rubbish bags, and the smells, and the tastes. Things that can and can't be eaten. Dangerous things, like broken glass. And danger from humans and dogs out for a late night walk. Cats on the prowl. Owls...

13 Think about the **characters** (p 41) the writer has created. Are they unusual in any way? What kinds of names do they have? Do they have a problem?

Unusual characters – foxes – a vixen and two cubs. Their names are unusual, not normal human names. A tod is the Scots word for a fox, so she is Mrs Fox. Mogs doesn't always do what he's told.

Problem – they are hungry and the cubs need to learn to find food and avoid danger.

14 What does the **plot** (p 45) seem to be, that is, what seems to be happening? What could happen next?

Mogs might learn that he likes pizza, Pixie might find some cat food. Mogs might go off exploring and get lost. They might meet a hedgehog, a mouse, a rat or other night creatures. Someone might come round with a bag of rubbish and disturb them. Another fox might chase them. They might meet their father...

We have read the passage, and the questions and answers have helped us to learn what the writer is doing. Read the passage again and then try the following Writer's Craft Task, using any of the above ideas, or ideas of your own.

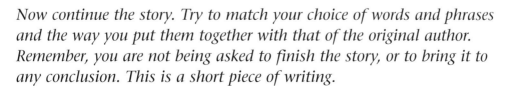 Writer's Craft Task

Now continue the story. Try to match your choice of words and phrases and the way you put them together with that of the original author. Remember, you are not being asked to finish the story, or to bring it to any conclusion. This is a short piece of writing.

Chapter 2

Practice Text
A Special Present

Now try a Writer's Craft Task on your own. You will find the
Fourteen Questions to Help You after the story. This time, you
have to answer them yourself.

Read the following story twice before you look at the questions.

I didn't mean it to turn out like THIS. I mean, it's Mum's
birthday and she DID say she wanted another cat. She collects
cats.

She's got LOTS of them already, mostly in the living room.
There are china cats on the shelves, glass cats on the windowsill
and furry cats on the sofa instead of cushions, but she hasn't got
a real live one yet.

"Robbie," I said to my best pal, "you know your cat, Elvis?"

"Yes, Alex?"

"You know how your wee sister hates cats and wants a dog
instead?"

"Yes…"

"Can I give Elvis to Mum for her birthday today?"

"OK."

We collected Elvis after school and Robbie carried him round
to my house. He is a big black cat with white paws and he
DIDN'T like being carried. He wriggled a lot and miaowed loudly.
He wasn't the kind of present you can wrap up, so we shut him
in the living room and waited in the kitchen for Mum to come
home. We were hungry.

"HAPPY BIRTHDAY!" we shouted, as she came in the back
door. She was carrying lots of bags of food which was a good
sign.

"Thank you, boys!" she said, with a BIG smile on her face.

Suddenly, there was a TERRIBLE crashing, smashing sound from behind the living-room door.

"What on EARTH is that?" Mum yelled, leaping in the air with fright and dropping the bags of food which made more crashing, smashing sounds as they landed on the floor.

Robbie and I just looked at each other as Mum went and opened the door of the living room.

Now answer the following questions with short notes: you don't need to write long sentences.

Fourteen Questions to Help You

1 What is this piece of writing about, that is, what is the subject of it? Maybe the title gives you a clue?

2 Why has the writer written it, that is, what is their purpose? To entertain you? To give you a particular feeling? To inform you? Something else?

3 Who is this story written for, that is, who do you feel is the audience for this story?

4 What kind of writing is it? Is it **imaginative writing**? (p 27) Is it **personal writing**? (p 27) Is it **functional writing**? (p 27) Can you say how you know this?

5 Does the writer use many **adjectives** (p 12) or **adverbs** (p 13)? Can you give two examples, from the passage, of an adjective and two of an adverb?

6 Can you see any **question marks** (p 15) or **exclamation marks** (p 16)? Why is the writer using them?

7 Does the writer use long, medium or short sentences or a mixture of all three? Do you see any *very* short sentences with only three or four words?

➔

Fourteen Questions to Help You **continued**

8   Do you see any patterns or repetitions in the writing? Why do you think the writer has done this?

9   Is the writer telling the story as if it has happened to them, using "I"? Or, is the writer narrating the story as if it has happened to someone else, using "he" or "she"?

10   Is the writer using any **direct speech** (p 22)?

11   Can you see any **similes** (p 92)? Can you quote one or two?

12   Has the writer **set the scene** (p 49) by describing the place where the story is happening? You are going to continue the story so can you think of anything that you could add to describe this place?

13   Think about the **characters** (p 41) the writer has created. Are they unusual in any way? What kinds of names do they have? Do they have a problem?

14   What does the **plot** (p 45) seem to be, that is, what seems to be happening? What could happen next?

You should now be ready to do your Writer's Craft Task for "A Special Present".

Writer's Craft Task

Now continue the story. Try to match your choice of words and phrases and the way you put them together with that of the original author. Remember, you are not being asked to finish the story, or to bring it to any conclusion. This is a short piece of writing.

Chapter 3

Practice Text
A Good Excuse

My name is Ben and I was late for school again this morning. I've now got a note for my mum from the teacher because that's the third time this week that I've been late. On Monday, I forgot my PE kit and had to go back for it. On Wednesday, I got a puncture in my front tyre when I was only halfway there and I had to push my bike the rest of the way to school.

But today, I had a really special reason.

I was cycling along the road, in good time, and I was pleased because I'd remembered to bring apples for our cookery class this afternoon. The road was quiet. On the left, the cliffs rose up high above me and, on the right, there was a drop through trees and brambles to the river far below.

I cycled round the bend and there in front of me, right in the middle of the road, was a huge swan. It was waddling towards me on big, black, webbed feet. When it saw me, it stopped. So did I.

It looked a bit lost. I knew it could only take off from water. If I left it there, it would probably get hit by a car. I didn't care about being late again because the swan was more important. It must have wandered up the slipway from the river a few hundred yards ahead of me.

Gently, I laid my bike down in the bushes at the side of the road, never taking my eyes off the swan. I started to walk slowly towards it. I got to about six feet away from it. It was the same height as me.

"Chssssss!" it hissed warningly at me.

I tried to forget that a swan is strong enough to break my arm with a blow from its wing.

→

"It's all right, swan, don't worry," I said quietly, trying to reassure it with my voice. "Just turn around and go back the way you came."

I spread my arms out slowly, like wings.

I took a step towards it. It hissed again, then lowered its head and turned away from me. It let me shepherd it along the road. I kept talking quietly to it and tried to keep it away from the middle of the road. It was a magnificent, big bird, with a black and orange beak, but it couldn't walk very quickly at all.

We were doing fine, the swan and I, until suddenly I heard the sound of a car coming along towards us from behind.

Writer's Craft Task

Now continue the story. Try to match your choice of words and phrases and the way you put them together with that of the original author. Remember, you are not being asked to finish the story, or to bring it to any conclusion. This is a short piece of writing.

You can use the Fourteen Questions to Help You (p 65) if you want.

Chapter 4

Practice Text
Casper the Hero

Once upon a time, in a beautiful lake, far, far away from here, there lived a snake. A water snake. A small, green, water snake. A small, green, water snake who possessed magical powers.

Casper the Water Snake, for that was his name, was as thin as a needle and as bright as an emerald. However, Casper could also transform himself into a water lily or a dragonfly or even a crocodile.

When he felt sleepy in the heat of the afternoon sun, he would blink his left eye once and become a water lily and rest on the surface of the lake, snoozing, drifting, as lazy insects droned quietly around him.

When he felt curious, he would left-blink twice into Casper the Dragonfly and soar high above the lake on lacy wings until he could see the whole world of lake and river and rainforest. From there, he could hear the birds calling and the monkeys chattering in the treetops.

When he felt afraid, he would left-blink three times and suddenly Casper the Crocodile would grunt and thrash his tail and open his huge, long snout to reveal dozens of sharp white teeth ready to attack or defend.

One beautiful morning, Casper the Dragonfly was curious. He was soaring above his lake, when he heard a strange noise. A roaring, tearing, screeching sound which came from no animal or bird he knew of. He flew swiftly towards the sound. He saw something which angered and terrified him. It was a machine. A big machine. A big, silver machine nearly as big as the chief's hut. A big, silver machine with long silver blades that flashed and whirled like swords in the sun.

→ The machine was slicing through the rainforest, towards Casper's lake. He buzzed closer until he could see a man with an evil smile driving this noisy, big, silver machine slowly through Casper's world, leaving a trail of broken trees and wounded plants behind him.

Casper wondered how to stop him. Should he stay as a dragonfly, or change to a crocodile?

Writer's Craft Task

Now continue the story. Try to match your choice of words and phrases and the way you put them together with that of the original author. Remember, you are not being asked to finish the story, or to bring it to any conclusion. This is a short piece of writing.

You can use the Fourteen Questions to Help You (p 65) if you want.

Chapter 5

Practice Text
No Ordinary Ghost

Kenneth and his little sister, Amy, lived in a village in the shade of a big mountain. All the houses were hundreds of years old and most of them had ghosts. These ghosts were friendly, silent and white, and glided around at twilight, going about their business from long ago.

"Do you think you can get ghosts that are not people?" Amy asked Kenneth one day.

"What do you mean?"

"Well, everyone's got men or women ghosts. They're boring! I'd like something more interesting."

"Like what? A ghost giraffe?"

"Don't be silly!" Amy laughed. "You don't get ghost giraffes."

"How do you know?"

"Well, do you?" Amy looked doubtful.

"Wait and see," Kenneth said in a spooky voice, waving his arms in the air.

That evening, as the sun set behind the mountain and twilight fell on the village, the usual pale ghosts began to drift quietly around inside their houses.

But in Kenneth and Amy's house, there was something else too.

"Listen!" said Amy. "What's that noise?"

It sounded like hobnailed boots, or perhaps hooves, echoing down the wooden stairs from the attic.

They ran out into the hall to see what it could be.

"Oh, my goodness!" shrieked Amy. "Look!"

Writer's Craft Task

Now continue the story. Try to match your choice of words and phrases and the way you put them together with that of the original author. Remember, you are not being asked to finish the story, or to bring it to any conclusion. This is a short piece of writing.

You can use the Fourteen Questions to Help You (p 65) if you want.

Chapter 6

Practice Text
The End of Term Play

Maria woke up, full of excitement. Today was the day she was starring in the school play. She had the part of Princess Serena and had more words to say than anyone else. Katie, her arch rival, only had the part of a frog and she didn't get to speak at all.

Maria had practised her lines for weeks now, and had spent the whole of last night going over and over them. What if she forgot the words in front of the whole school and her parents? That would be the worst thing ever.

"Maria? Are you awake?" her mum called. "Time to get up."

Maria opened her mouth to say that she was already awake and just about to get up, but no sound came out. She swallowed hard and tried again. Nothing! Her voice had vanished! Her throat hurt too, now that she came to think about it. She leapt out of bed in disbelief. She had to star in the play today. She just had to!

"Maria?" her mum called again.

Maria heard her mum coming upstairs to see why she hadn't replied.

Writer's Craft Task

Now continue the story. Try to match your choice of words and phrases and the way you put them together with that of the original author. Remember, you are not being asked to finish the story, or to bring it to any conclusion. This is a short piece of writing.

You can use the Fourteen Questions to Help You (p 65) if you want.

Chapter 7

Practice Text
The Outer Edges

Spetrik, at only eight years old, was one of the youngest ever to pass the Junior Rocket Test. Most of the rest of the Junior Fleet were at least 11, but Spetrik's father-man was Senior Fleet Commander. He had more than 1000 rocket-men and rocket-women under his command. Spetrik had accompanied his father-man on many star-missions and, although it was against planet Meslania's rules, he had even piloted the Senior Fleet's star-rocket, while sitting on his father-man's lap.

So Spetrik had already tasted the freedom of whizzing at twice the speed of time through super-space, of spiralling through the fiery, orange rings around the dead planet of Lykora, and of racing towards the outer edges of super-space, beyond which lay the Unexplored Zones.

Spetrik sent a tele-thought to his best-pal-boy, Brisker.

"Hey, Space Kid, Junior Rocket Boy here! I passed! Fancy a spin to the outer edges?"

"Yeah, Spetrik Rocket Boy! Does your father-man know you're going?"

"Neah, but we'll be back before eat-time and he'll never know."

"I'm with you, Rocket Boy! Can you come and collect me? Hover at my sleep-capsule window, because mother-woman's mad at me and won't let me out."

"Why's your mother-woman mad at you?"

"I broke the star-catcher and we've had no light for three sun-sweeps now."

"OK, Space Kid, I'll be with you in 10 pytes. How did you break the star-catcher anyway?"

Writer's Craft Task

Now continue the story. Try to match your choice of words and phrases and the way you put them together with that of the original author. Remember, you are not being asked to finish the story, or to bring it to any conclusion. This is a short piece of writing.

You can use the Fourteen Questions to Help You (p 65) if you want.

Chapter 8

Practice Text
About these Trainers...

Dear Sir/Madam,

I am writing to complain about a pair of trainers I bought in your shop yesterday. There were lots of problems, which are not yet over.

First, I had to wait for 20 minutes before someone was prepared to serve me. The shop wasn't even busy.

Second, your assistant took another 10 minutes to fetch a pair of trainers for me to try on. She seemed very bored and she brought me the wrong size and the wrong colour. It was more than an hour before I could leave the shop with my new trainers.

I was wanting to wear them yesterday evening, for running practice, but when I got home and opened the box I couldn't believe my eyes.

Writer's Craft Task

Now continue this letter. Try to match your choice of words and phrases and the way you put them together with that of the original author. Remember, you are not being asked to finish the letter, or to bring it to any conclusion. This is a short piece of writing.

You can use the Fourteen Questions to Help You (p 65) if you want.

Chapter 9

Practice Text
Bananas!

My diary, Monday, 25th August.

I came home from school today and found this really rude note from Mum waiting for me on the kitchen table.

"Lily – because you never help in the house, today you are going to make pudding for all four of us. Here's what to do. Make sure it's ready for six o-clock…"

There was this great long list of orders, telling me what to do and what not to do! She gets so mad at me when I leave the freezer door open even a little, and she hates me throwing things at the bin, though I don't usually miss. She won't let me dry my hands on the dish towel or give the cat, who is honestly not very fat, some extra treats. She's so fussy!

Anyway, the kitchen was like a bombsite with dirty dishes everywhere and a huge pile of dirty washing on the floor. She expected me to prepare bananas and cream and chocolate sprinkles and stuff. I hate bananas!

So I decided I wasn't going to. I didn't care! I have better things to do. I left her a note.

Writer's Craft Task

Now continue the story. Try to match your choice of words and phrases and the way you put them together with that of the original author. Remember, you are not being asked to finish the story, or to bring it to any conclusion. This is a short piece of writing.

You can use the Fourteen Questions to Help You (p 65) if you want.

Chapter 10

Practice Text
Pat the Cat

Pat is a cat. Pat is a hungry cat. Pat is looking for food.

Pat looks on the chair. He sees a cushion. Pat shakes his head. Cats don't eat cushions.

Pat looks under the chair. He sees a shoe. Pat shakes his head. Cats don't eat shoes.

Pat looks on the table. He sees a book. Pat shakes his head. Cats don't eat books.

Pat looks under the table. He sees a rug. Pat shakes his head. Cats don't eat rugs.

Writer's Craft Task

Now continue the story. Try to match your choice of words and phrases and the way you put them together with that of the original author. Remember, you are not being asked to finish the story, or to bring it to any conclusion. This is a short piece of writing.

You can use the Fourteen Questions to Help You (p 65) if you want.

Part Three

Stories, Poems and Pictures to Inspire You

Chapter 11

Age Concern

This poem is fun to read aloud. It is like a very short play with two characters. Find a partner and read it aloud and take turns to be either the granny or the grandchild.

Age Concern

Happy birthday, Granny!
What age are you now?

Just a year older than last year.

What age is that, Granny?

A bit younger than the Queen.

But she's dead old, Granny!

*Well, actually, I'm a couple
of years older than Sophia Loren.*

Are you sure, Granny? What age is she?

Just slightly younger than Pavarotti.

Oh! Granny! Are you as old as that?

Well, if you can keep a secret,
I'll tell you… I'm the same age
as Mickey Mouse…

Awwwh! Granny!
I knew you were just young.

Teresa McCluskey

Questions

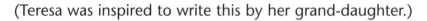

(Teresa was inspired to write this by her grand-daughter.)

1 What age do you think the grandchild might be?

2 Why do you think this?

3 How does Granny try to avoid giving her real age?

4 Why do you think she might not want to say how old she is?

5 How do you feel about being the age you are now?

6 The title is clever for two reasons. The first is because the grandchild is concerned about Granny's age. Do you know what else Age Concern is? See if you can find out. When a writer deliberately uses two meanings at the same time, we say they are "making a pun".

7 Try to find out when the Queen was born.

8 Who are (or were) Sophia Loren and Pavarotti? If you don't already know, try to find this out and also try to find out when they were born.

Questions continued

9 The ending is clever because the grandchild thinks she finally knows how "young" Granny is. What age does she think Granny is? Has Granny *really* given away her age? See if you can find out both how old, and how young, Mickey Mouse is.

10 How do you think the grandmother and her grand-daughter feel about each other? Why do you think this?

A Closer Look at Teresa McCluskey's Writing Skills

Using punctuation and type styles to create characters

Teresa has used normal type for the grandchild's words and sloping italic type for Granny's words. (Italic type is called this because it was an *Italian* who invented it, more than 500 years ago. His name was Aldo Manuzio.)

1 Read only the grandchild's words (in normal type) and make a list of each punctuation mark Teresa uses and how many times she uses it.

2 Now read only Granny's words (in italic type) and, again, make a list of each punctuation mark and how many times Teresa uses it. (The three dots (…) are called an ellipsis.)

3 Teresa uses an ellipsis twice, to show that Granny is pausing and hesitating. Why do you think Granny is doing this?

4 Judging by the words and the punctuation marks, how are these two characters (Granny and the grandchild) very different?

5 How does the very last punctuation mark in the poem make this remark different from the grandchild's other lines? Why do you think this is?

Using a pattern

When you look at this poem on the page you can see that Teresa has used patterns to make it easier for us to understand.

1 She has used two different type styles to separate the two characters. How else has Teresa laid out the poem on the page so that we can see clearly how Granny and the grandchild are taking turns at speaking?

2 Can you think of any other ways the poem could be laid out, or any other type styles Teresa could have used, to separate her two characters?

3 There is another pattern within Granny's answers that you will have to look closely to find. (Hint: look at the way Teresa uses the words "older" and "younger".) Can you see what this is?

Clever Ideas That You Can Use Too

1 Using punctuation and type styles to create characters

2 Using a pattern

3 Making up a clever title with a pun

4 Reaching a clever ending

Four Ideas For Your Own Writing

Idea 1

Teresa has written a question-and-answer poem. She has created a curious grandchild, and a loving grandmother who is trying gently not to reveal her age. Granny gives answers that are only half-answers, answers that are like riddles, even at the end.

Think of a question you, or someone else, might not want to answer. Perhaps your grandfather might not want to say how old he is? Or you might not want to tell your mum or dad what you've been up to? Or you might not want to say exactly where you've been? Or where you are going for your holidays? Or how much pocket money you get? Or…?

Then, think of several ways of avoiding answering the question, of not giving a straight answer. You'll need at least three answers, but try to think of several more, so you can choose the best ones.

Now, using Teresa's poem as a model, write your own poem, with questions and answers. Give it a good title.

Idea 2

Earlier, in question 5, you were asked how you felt about being your age. Let's use your answer to that as a starting point.

Make a list of the really good things about being your age. Make another list of the really bad things about being your age. Try to think of at least six different ideas for each list.

If you want to find ideas, think about what you can and can't do now, and about what you have and can't have now. You can compare your life when you were younger with your life now, and you can think about your hopes and your fears for when you are older.

Now edit your two lists down to three items on each list. Choose the best, the most unusual, the funniest, the worst items. Ask a writing partner to help you choose, if you are not sure.

Now you have choices about how to make a pattern. Here is one way:

What is bad about being my age?

What is good about being my age?

What is worse?

What is better?

What is the worst?

What is the best?

You can write in your own answers to complete the poem.

Or, you can go back to your first lists and choose to write about only the good things or only the bad things.

Or, you can make up different questions.

Or, you can try to take away the questions and see if only your answers still make a good poem.

Experiment... this is the only way to be creative and imaginative.

Idea 3

Write about one or more of your grandparents. How are they different from your parents? Do you behave differently when you are with them? How do they treat you? Can you describe them? What do they look like? How do they move? What is their home like? Are there any scents or smells that make you think of them? Any colours? Any sounds? Any hobbies they have? Anything else that you can think of?

You can write this either as a poem or as a piece of personal writing.

Idea 4

How do you feel about maybe being a grandparent some day? Write about what you think might be good, and what might be bad? What would you like your grandchildren to be? How would you like them to treat you? How many grandchildren would you like to have? Anything else you can think of?

You can write this either as a poem or as a piece of personal writing.

Picture 1

Use this picture to inspire you to write a story or a poem or a memory or a hope.

You can write about it in whatever way you wish, but it might help you to think about the following 8 questions. (There are no wrong answers...)

1   What does this seem to be?

2   What else might it be?

3   Who or what might be connected to this?

4   Where might it be?

5   When?

6   Who or what else might be involved?

7   What could happen next?

8   What sounds, smells or feelings could there be?

Chapter 12

The Stag

The Stag

Joe and I were playing cards and Mum was making tea when we heard the news on the telly:

"Earlier this evening, a window was smashed at a restaurant in Orchid Street. It is thought that a stag..."

We were out the front door and on the bus in two minutes. We jumped off at the stop on the corner of Orchid Street and the High Street. Orchid Street was blocked off with yellow tapes but we could see a crowd outside the River Café so we got under the tapes and legged it up there. The people were standing behind more yellow tapes, and there were two policemen.

I saw this big brown shape on the pavement and I knew what it was right away.

It was only yesterday we skipped school at dinnertime and saw the stag. We skip sometimes, Joe and I. Just say, "Home dinner!" to Miss Cleckton when she takes the register and then keep the dinner money for chips and sweets. Easy.

Anyway, Joe'd been reading in the local paper about the deer coming further and further into the city, getting in people's gardens and eating their plants, and he was crazy to see one close up. Mad about anything with four legs, Joe is.

So I couldn't believe it when we were walking down to the grass bit where we go to eat our chips and this huge creature comes racing across the road ahead of us. At first I thought it was a great big dog but then I saw the antlers. We had to jump back as the car swerved to miss it and the tyres whined and screeched.

→

It bounded right in front of us and dashed for the trees at the back of the clearing.

"Shh," whispered Joe, "let's follow. Don't make no noise."

We crept towards the trees, trying not to step on the bits of twig which were snapping under our feet, and we hadn't gone more than a few yards when we saw him.

He was big, sort of proud-looking with these huge spread-out antlers like great big branches on his head. He was greyish brown with a white face and throat and black tips to his ears. His neck and chest were still panting after his run. He didn't seem to know we were there and stood still, just jerking his head from side to side like he was listening.

Joe wasn't hardly breathing.

"E's a beauty," he whispered.

When we got outside the River Café and saw the glass in a thousand pieces on the pavement and the big shape lying there, Joe went all stiff.

"It's 'im," he said.

Some men put him on a stretcher and lifted him up on to a truck. He was lying on his side and we could see his head was all cut and bloody. He had his eyes open but they were all blank and white, like a cloud was over them.

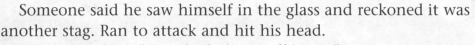

→ Someone said he saw himself in the glass and reckoned it was another stag. Ran to attack and hit his head.

"Come on, Joey," I said, "let's get off 'ome."

Alexandra Power

Questions

1 Why do you think Joe and the narrator rushed off to Orchid Street?

2 How do you think they were feeling?

3 It is unusual for deer to come into cities. Can you think of any reasons why this might happen? (There is a hint in the local paper.)

4 How did the two boys know it wasn't "a great big dog"?

5 Quote the three sounds that Alexandra uses in the middle of her story to make it work better.

6 Alexandra describes the stag in the trees in the paragraph beginning, "He was big, sort of proud-looking…". What simile (p 92) does she use here to describe his antlers? Do you think this is a good simile? Why?

7 Quote three more details that she uses in this paragraph to make us see the stag clearly.

8 How does Alexandra contrast the way the stag and Joe are each breathing in the trees? Why is each breathing this way?

9 The second time Alexandra describes the stag, in the last section, he is very different. What simile does she use here to describe his eyes? Do you think this is a good simile? Why?

10 Why do you think the narrator calls Joe "Joey" at the end?

→

Questions continued

11 How does the stag's encounter with the car hint at what is going to happen to him later?

12 Can you think of any wild animals or birds that have come into our cities from wilder places and now live successfully alongside us?

A Closer Look at Alexandra Power's Writing Skills

Creating effective similes

When we compare two things that are similar in some way, and when we use the word "like" or "as", we are creating a simile.

Alexandra uses two excellent similes to help us see the stag's antlers and the stag's eyes more clearly.

Let's say we wanted to describe the colour of a cat's eyes. We could say:

> The cat's eyes were blue.

But if we use a simile, our description can be improved:

> The cat's eyes were *like* sapphires.
>
> The cat's eyes were *as* blue *as* sapphires.

Here, the *colour* (and sparkle) of the cat's eyes are similar to the *colour* (and sparkle) of a sapphire. In other ways (shape, texture, temperature, use), cats' eyes are very different from sapphires.

Here are some more simple statements:

The startled frog jumped.

The canoe cut through the water.

The sea was cold.

The custard slithered out the jug.

Her hair was pink.

The explosion was loud.

The autumn leaves turned pale.

Here they are again, but with similes to improve the description.

> The startled frog jumped *like* a kangaroo.
>
> The canoe cut through the water *like* a knife.
>
> The sea was *as* cold *as* ice.
>
> The custard slithered out the jug *like* a thick, yellow snake.
>
> Her hair was *as* pink *as* a radish.
>
> The explosion was *as* loud *as* thunder.
>
> The autumn leaves turned *as* pale *as* butter.

If you use similes they will make your writing more vivid. Quite often there is a bit of exaggeration in a simile too.

Later in your English studies, but not in this book, you will look more closely at other ways of comparing things too.

Using a flashback

This story is in three parts. Look again at only the middle part (from "It was only yesterday..." to "... he whispered."). It is almost a complete story on its own.

Now read only the first and last parts. If you read them without the middle part, they are almost a complete story too. Why do we need both parts to make the story complete?

If we think about the time-line that Alexandra has used to structure her story, we can see that the story starts today when the boys hear news about a stag, then moves to yesterday when the boys saw the stag, then moves back to a little later today when they realise that the stag which they saw yesterday is the same one that has now died. So we could write her time-line this way:

Today – yesterday – later today.

Alexandra could have started with yesterday and told the story in the order in which it happened. But instead, she has created suspense by stopping the today-story just when we want to know more, and giving us the yesterday-story which makes us even more curious to know what has happened.

So, Alexandra uses a flashback not only to tell us about the boys seeing the stag the day before, but also to make us want to read on.

Have you ever used a flashback in your writing? Can you think of any stories, books, films or television programmes where the writer uses a flashback?

Including a range of emotions, from happy to sad

If we are aware of emotions, or feelings, we can use them to make our writing better. It can help to make our readers feel things too.

We can use two opposite emotions to make our writing even more powerful. For example, this story uses both happiness and sadness. In the first part, the boys rush off to Orchid Street feeling concerned and worried. In the second part, they are excited and amazed to see a real stag close-up. In the third part, they are sad because "their" stag has died.

You can also find Edwin Morgan using happiness and sadness in "Red Deer" (p 98).

If each writer had used only one emotion, then their writing would have been less effective. Behind this is the idea of contrast, of balancing happiness against sadness. It is said that we need to know what happiness is, before we can know what sadness is, and that we need to know what cold is, before we can understand warm fully. Do you agree with this?

Clever Ideas That You Can Use Too

1 Creating effective similes

2 Using a flashback

3 Including a range of emotions, from happy to sad

Three Ideas For Your Own Writing

Idea 1

Joe and the narrator ran out of the house without telling their mum where they were going. Write about what happens when they return home for tea. Think about how they are feeling. How will they explain this to their mum? Remember that they were skipping school when they first saw the stag.

Idea 2

These two boys have had a close encounter with wild animal. Write about an encounter you have had with an animal or bird, wild or tame, and try to use at least two similes to describe how it looks, moves, sounds or smells. If you can write about how you and the animal react to each other, then you will find it easier than just describing it. If you can include conflict (see p 44) and emotions, then your writing will be even better. You might also want to try to include a flashback.

Idea 3

Deer were first mentioned in the local paper, in Alexandra's story. Write a newspaper report about the events in Orchid Street for the first page of the next edition of the local paper. You can invent more details about it, and include interviews with people who were there, perhaps in the restaurant, or on the street. Perhaps the boys might be included or anyone else who was involved, like the police or the men with the truck, or a vet.

Once you've written your story, design the front page of the newspaper too – giving it a name and using different typesizes for this name and for the headline. Include illustrations if you can.

Picture 2

Use this picture to inspire you to write a story or a poem or a memory or a hope.

You can write about it in whatever way you wish, but it might help you to think about the following 8 questions. (There are no wrong answers…)

1   What does this seem to be?
2   What else might it be?
3   Who or what might be connected to this?
4   Where might it be?
5   When?
6   Who or what else might be involved?
7   What could happen next?
8   What sounds, smells or feelings could there be?

Chapter 13

Red Deer

Red Deer

We are the deer
and we are here.
We like it here.
We couple and we fight,
eat everything in sight,
and some say that's not right.
We're nearly half a million strong:
suppose we ran in unison,
gliding like a spreading stain
across the windy high terrain,
who could cull us, who could kill us,
smell of stalkers couldn't chill us.
– That's a dream we sometimes dream
beside the falls and roaring stream,
and then we wake to rifle-cracks
and feel the kitchen at our backs.
Brothers, get those antlers clashing!
Bellow if the rain is lashing!
Sisters, trot through bog and heather,
take dainty fill of every weather!
Ears cocked, nostrils flared,
browse and watch, don't be scared.
Watch and browse, green delight,
shoots and roots, soon comes night,
soon comes snow
when you must go

→

starving and gaunt
downhill to haunt
the homes of men.
What then, what then?

Edwin Morgan

Make sure you know the meaning of these words: unison, terrain, cull, stalkers, dainty fill, flared, browse, gaunt. Use a dictionary to help you.

Then read this poem again. Read it together, aloud, as if you were the herd of deer.

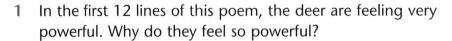

Questions

1. In the first 12 lines of this poem, the deer are feeling very powerful. Why do they feel so powerful?

2. The poem changes in line 13. What one word in this line changes the power in the first 12 lines?

3. What does "…and then we wake to rifle-cracks / and feel the kitchen at our backs" mean?

4. Look again at the last six lines. Why are the deer forced down from the hills? What one word in these lines best explains this?

5. What do you think could be an answer to the question in the last line?

6. Why is "haunt" such a clever word to use?

7. Edwin has used rhyme (p 36–39) in his poem. By looking at the last word in each line, can you work out what rhyming scheme (p 37) he has used?

8. Look more closely at the last two lines. What has he done with his rhyme here? Why do you think he has done this?

9. Can you see at least three other lines where he has rhyming words *inside* the lines too? We call this internal rhyme.

Now that you have looked closely at this poem, read the poem aloud again, together, using the volume of your voices (loud or quiet), and your tone of voice (happy or sad), and the pace (quick or slow) to dramatise it.

A Closer Look at Edwin Morgan's Writing Skills

Making patterns with shape, rhyme and rhythm

Teresa's poem, "Age Concern" (p 82), uses a pattern. Edwin has used a pattern here too. How would you describe the shape of his poem on the page?

His poem is in two parts, separated by a dash at the start of a line. How else could Edwin have separated these two parts?

We have already looked at the rhyming scheme, but Edwin also uses rhythm (p 32–36). Read the first three short lines aloud. The rhythm in these lines, which all rhyme, is very short and quick, as if the deer were standing still, stamping their feet for emphasis.

Read the next three longer lines aloud. These lines, which also rhyme, have a more bouncy rhythm, with more words and more movement in the deer.

Read the next six lines. These six lines, which are even longer and which use three rhymes, have a very strong rhythm, like hundreds of thousands of deer running over the hillsides.

So Edwin has used line length and rhyme deliberately to create different rhythms.

Can you also see one simile (p 92) in these lines?

All of this – the shape, the two parts, the rhyme and the rhythm – are deliberate. And they all make the poem work better.

Using personification

Edwin writes this poem as if he *were* the deer speaking: "We are the deer…". Deer can't speak but Edwin is pretending that they are like people and can speak. We call this personification.

This is used a lot in cartoons (for example, in Mickey Mouse, *The Jungle Book*, and *Finding Nemo*) and in stories for young children (for example, in *The Three Bears, Little Red Riding Hood* and *The Gruffalo*). In all of these, there are creatures that are not human and cannot speak, which are personified and given voices as if they were human. Can you think of any other examples of personification you've seen or read?

Clever Ideas That You Can Use Too

1　Writing a poem or a story in two parts, with a big change in the middle

2　Using line length, and shape on the page, in your poems

3　Using rhythm and rhyme

4　Using personification

Four Ideas For Your Own Writing

Idea 1

Edwin imagines he is a deer and writes his poem from their point of view (p 39–41). He uses a good dream (power) and a bad reality (starvation). Choose a different animal or bird, one that can have a good dream and bad reality (or a nightmare then a good reality). This might involve cages or traps or suffering of some sort... Write your own poem as if you were that animal, using "I". You can use layout and line length to help you. And rhythm and rhyme, if you want, too.

Idea 2

There is a vast graveyard in the middle of Glasgow called the Necropolis (this is a Latin word that means Death-City). It is so big that not only do some homeless people live there in the old tombs, but two deer (a mother and her fawn) have also lived there for several years now. Write about what you think living in a graveyard in the middle of a city might be like, for either a person or some other creature that has set up home there. Think about daytime and night-time, and about the tourists (or relatives) who might come to visit. What do you think would be the best and worst things about this way of life? If you prefer to make up a story set in a graveyard, do that instead, or as well!

Idea 3

You will need to do some research for this next writing idea which connects to environmental studies. See if you can find out why the deer are starving in the first place. See if you can also find out what solutions we are trying to find for this problem. Write an article about this, explaining the reasons for the problem and the possible solutions. What do you think should be done? Why?

Idea 4

See if you can also find out about other wild birds or animals that are moving into our cities and succeeding in making their homes there. How are we creating environments that are not unlike the ones they would have in their normal wild habitat? Write a report on one of these creatures, explaining what it is, where and how it normally lives in the wild, and where and how it now also lives in cities.

Links Between "Red Deer" and "The Stag"

Please make sure you have read both this poem and this story, before you read any further.

Deer are moving more into the places where people live, whether villages or cities. This fact has inspired both Alexandra and Edwin, but they have each chosen to write about it in a very different way.

Alexandra has written a story about two boys who see a stag in the city, which then dies fighting itself. Can you find the short sentence near the end of her story where she describes her stag fighting himself? Can you find the exclamation in Edwin's poem that also describes deer fighting?

You can see how both writers use rhythm if you look at this short sentence of Alexandra's again, and also read the *first* two lines of Edwin's poem again. The rhythm in these two short sentences is remarkably similar. Each writer wants to emphasise, to surprise us, to shock us. You too can use short sentences for effect, now and again, and it will improve your writing. How well do you think your writing would work if you used short sentences all the time?

Alexandra and Edwin also both write about deer needing to come down from their hills to find enough food. Can you find the part where Alexandra writes about this (it's in the middle section of her story) and the way Edwin writes about this near the end of his poem?

These two very different ways of saying the same thing about deer starving show you the difference between writing a story and writing a poem. In the poem, the same information is given as in the story, but using rhythm and rhyme instead.

The point of the poem is not just to give you information, but to make it sound good to the ear, and to give us pictures in our head ("… snow… gaunt…haunt…") to play with the information, to transform it by making it into a poem.

The point of the story is to involve us in the lives of the narrator and Joe, and of the stag. Both writers want to make us feel sympathy for deer. How well do you think each has done this?

Does Alexandra's story in any way suggest answers to the question in the last line of Edwin's poem?

Picture 3

Use this picture to inspire you to write a story or a poem or a memory or a hope.

You can write about it in whatever way you wish, but it might help you to think about the following 8 questions. (There are no wrong answers...)

1   What does this seem to be?

2   What else might it be?

3   Who or what might be connected to this?

4   Where might it be?

5   When?

6   Who or what else might be involved?

7   What could happen next?

8   What sounds, smells or feelings could there be?

Chapter 14

Tigger

Tigger

Tigger's no the most original name for a cat, but I was only eight when I got him. I'd really wanted a dog but Mum and Dad said we'd nae room and it wouldnae be fair tae get wan. And a dog would be a lot of work too. I didnae know that my mum was gonnae have my wee brother then, of course. Danny. He's three now.

Tigger's three and a half but wan year of a cat's life is like seven years of a human's so that makes him twenty-four-and-a-half-year auld. He's orange and stripy and has big long legs, just like Tigger in the cartoon. He's no like other cats. He's a bit wild, likes tae go hunting outside; sometimes he's away all day, but he always comes hame. I put his food down for him just before we have wur tea, then I go oot the back and whistle, a special whistle only I can dae; and he just appears, from naewhere. I don't know any other cats that dae that. And every night he sleeps on my bed curled up at the bottom, purring away.

When I first got him he was six week auld, a wee bundle of orange fur wi big yellow eyes. Mum tried tae make him sleep downstair. She got a bed for him and put in a hot-water bottle and an alarm clock wrapped up in a blanket. That's supposed tae make the kitten think it's his mother's heartbeat. But Tigger wasnae having any of that. He kept coming up the stair, trying tae get intae my room. He shouted at the door. I don't mean mewed or yowled or any of the normal things cats dae; I mean he shouted, just like a person. Then when nothing happened he started throwing hisself at the door, really throwing hisself hard

→

and scratching wi his claws on the way down, like a cartoon cat.
And he never got fed up wi it, he went on and on and on till
finally Mum had tae gie in and let him sleep in my room. A lot
of folk think that cats are no as good as dogs; they don't dae
tricks and they're kind of girlie pets, but Tigger's no like that.
He's wild like a dog but he's my cat cause he only comes for me.
He's my best pal.

And now Mum wants me tae get rid of him.

It was yesterday she tellt me. It would of been bad enough but
I wisht she hadnae done it that way. See, she took me oot for my
tea, just me and her, tae the café. We used tae dae that when I
was wee, afore Danny came along, once a week when my Dad
was working shifts and wasnae always hame at teatime. It was
our special treat she always said. We'd have egg and chips and
tattie scones and I had beans too but Mum doesnae like them.
Anyway we never went for a while efter Danny was born cause it
was too much bother she said, then when we started tae go again
it wasnae the same cause Danny's always stealing my chips –
even though he has a plate of his own he always wants mines.
I dae mair things with my Dad on my ain noo; he takes me tae
the footie and we go fishing sometimes.

Anyhow, when Mum and me went tae the café last night it
was dead good; just the two of us, sitting in the windae without
Danny gaun on and on every time a truck or a bus went by, or
chucking his food about. The café was warm and noisy and when
we'd finished wur food Mum said, "I want tae talk tae you about
something important, Joe."

I looked at her face, wondering what was coming next.
I thought for a minute she was gonnae tell me she was having
another baby, but she looked so serious I knew it couldnae be
that.

"It's about Danny."

"Danny? Is something wrang?"

Danny had been gaun for tests at the hospital for a few month
now. He gets hay fever and has eczema on his skin too. The
doctors were trying tae find oot what was causing it.

Mum said, "The doctors think he might be allergic tae something. If you're allergic tae something you have reactions tae it, maybe a rash or being sick. It can be something ordinary that doesnae affect most people."

My mum sometimes explains things tae me as if I'm five.

"I know what allergic means, Mum. David McSween's allergic tae peanuts – he comes oot in big lumps if he even touches wan. He has tae carry adrenaline about wi him in case he eats wan by accident."

"That's terrible. Danny's no as bad as that, thank goodness. But the doctors have said he has tae stop drinking milk and eating cheese."

Danny won't like that. He's practically addicted tae thae wee cheese triangles, the ones that come wrapped up in silver foil. He spreads them on his toast in the morning and puts marmalade on top – yeuch.

"And there's a few other things too. Like Tigger."

"Tigger?"

"See, they think that Tigger's fur could be affecting Danny – well, no his fur exactly, just some wee mites that live in it."

I was furious. "Tigger doesnae have fleas. He wears a flea collar, I gie him that flea powder every summer. And he's the cleanest cat you ever seen. He's always washing hisself."

"Joe, it's nothing tae dae wi being clean. All cats have wee insects that live in their fur – they're that toty you cannae see them, and normally they don't dae any harm. But some people, like Danny, are affected by them. So I'm asking you tae help oot with this. For Danny."

Just then, my ice cream arrived; vanilla, wi a flake and raspberry sauce. My favourite. I put the spoon intae the ice cream but it was still quite hard. I only managed tae get a wee bit on the spoon. I put it on my tongue, letting it melt there.

"It's OK, Mum. I'll keep Tigger oot of Danny's way. I could feed him outside and no let him into the house except at night-time. And I'll wait tae Danny's in his bed and carry him up the stairs tae my room. Danny doesnae need tae have anything tae dae wi him."

Mum stirred her coffee. "Joe, I'm sorry, son, I don't think that'll be enough."

"What?"

"I'm asking you tae let us find a new hame for Tigger."

The ice cream tasted sour in my mouth, like milk that's gone off. I didnae know whit tae say. Mum reached over the table and touched my airm.

"It's OK son, you don't have tae decide just now. And I'm no gonnae force you. It's your decision."

When we got hame, Danny was sitting in his pyjamas, watching a video, haudin his teddy, the special wan he takes tae bed. He used tae have loads of cuddlies; he'd fill the bed wi hedgehogs and bunnies and all sorts, but the doctor said they might be causing the allergies so now he's only got wan. When Mum came in, he ran tae her and she lifted him and cairried him up the stair tae his bed. His pyjamas rode up tae the knee and I could see the red patches on his legs, sore and weeping. He has special ointment tae put on it but it's still really itchy and horrible.

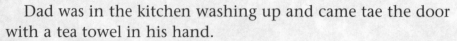

Dad was in the kitchen washing up and came tae the door with a tea towel in his hand.

"OK. Joe?"

"Aye, fine, Dad."

"Enjoy your tea?"

"Yeah. Did Tigger get his?"

"About an hour ago. He's away oot again."

I went tae the back door and whistled my special whistle. It was starting tae get dark and the shadows at the back of the garden flickered as if they were alive. I kept thinking I could see Tigger but it was the light tricking my eyes. I whistled again. Sometimes it took him a while tae get back from wherever he'd been. A wee yowl, a soft shape against my leg and there he was. I picked him up and he rubbed hisself round my neck, purring, his throat vibrating.

That night I lay awake in my bed, Tigger asleep at my feet, as usual. I couldnae imagine what it would be like no tae have him there – a couple of times he'd stayed out all night and I couldnae sleep; no really worried about him cause he's the kind of cat who can take care of hisself, just no feeling right if I couldnae hear his breathing in the night or see his faint outline in the dark at the foot of the bed. And what would it be like no tae wake up wi him licking my face or watch him come hame when I whistle for him?

It would be different if Danny was gonnae die or something. I know that sounds terrible, but I saw a video once about a boy who gave up one of his kidneys for his brother and if Mum had asked me tae dae that I wouldnae even think about it – I'd dae it right away. I mean you only need wan kidney. And tae see your brother having tae get wired up tae a machine three days a week and no be able tae dae anything, well, that's terrible. But Danny's no seriously ill. I mean he gets a bit stuffed up and his eyes run and all that, but that happens tae loads of folk. And I know eczema's horrible and sometimes he cries because it's sore, but still, it's no fair tae ask me tae get rid of Tigger. I bet they wouldnae ask him tae dae it.

What was it Mum had said? "I won't force you. It's your decision." How can I make a decision like that? I wisht she'd just said we're getting rid of him, then I wouldnae have tae decide. I could just blame them. But then, I wouldnae have Tigger.

I moved myself round in the bed so I was lying with my heid at the foot of it, just beside him. I put my foreheid against his back and felt his soft fur, tickly against my nose. Tigger always smells of outside, of grass and earth and leaves. He never opened his eyes but he jerked a bit in his sleep and started tae purr, loudly, his whole body vibrating against my heid.

Maybe I could just wait, see if this no drinking milk helps Danny, maybe I could keep Tigger outside; he could sleep in the shed. At least I'd know he was there, close by. Maybe that would be enough.

Anne Donovan

Questions

1 Joe has a special relationship with Tigger. Look in the second paragraph of the story and, in your own words, give two examples of how well they get on.

2 Quote the one short sentence in paragraph 3 that sums up this relationship.

3 In what ways did Joe's relationship with his mum change after Danny was born?

4 What do you think Joe felt he gained and lost?

5 Why does Joe wish his mum hadn't taken him out for tea to tell him about Danny's allergy to Tigger?

6 Why is Joe pleased that Danny isn't in the café with them? List three things that Danny does which annoy Joe.

7 Why do you think Joe's mum explains to Joe about allergies as if he were five?

Questions continued

8 Why does Joe get "furious"?

9 What does his mum then say that makes the ice cream suddenly taste so sour?

10 Why do you think she wants Joe to decide what happens to Tigger?

11 How do you think Joe feels about Danny? What details in the story tell you this?

12 Look at the second last paragraph. By which smells, sensations and emotions does Joe know Tigger?

13 In the last paragraph, Anne uses the word "maybe" three times and we are not sure what happens next. What do you think happens next? Why do you think this?

14 Is there anything in the story that suggests to you that Tigger might make up his own mind, even if Joe does decide to give him away?

A Closer Look at Anne Donovan's Writing Skills

Using very short sentences and paragraphs for effect.

Look again at the length of the first five paragraphs on page 106–107. You will notice that the fourth paragraph is extremely short – in fact, it is the shortest paragraph, apart from dialogue, in the whole story. The last sentence of the third paragraph is also extremely short.

Anne has done this deliberately to make her writing work better. First, she writes three paragraphs about how much Joe loves Tigger, summing it up with the very short, simple sentence, "He's my best pal."

She then takes a new paragraph, because this is a big turning point in the story, "And now Mum wants me tae get rid of him." It is such a dramatic change, that it deserves a paragraph to itself.

The story then changes into flashback, moving back to yesterday, when Joe learned about the terrible decision he is going to have to make.

Most sentences and paragraphs in stories are not noticeably long or short. This means that a writer can occasionally use very short sentences or paragraphs to make a dramatic point stand out clearly. You too can use this in your writing to make it more powerful.

Creating a character through the way they speak

Anne has decided to tell this story from the point of view of Joe, an 11-year-old boy.

You will have noticed that some of the words and spellings she has used are not in standard English. For example, "Tigger's no the most original name... Mum and Dad said we'd nae room and it wouldnae be fair tae get wan... I didnae know that my mum was gonnae have my wee brother then..."

Anne has done this to capture the way the wee boy speaks. This helps to create the character of Joe. Try "translating" the three short extracts in the paragraph above into standard English. What has happened to Joe's character?

You too can do this, either in the main part of a story, or within the dialogue. The secret is to change the spelling of only a few words, not every single word, and to keep the same spelling each time.

Using all five senses

Anne makes good use of all five senses to characterise both Joe and Tigger more fully.
She tells us what Tigger looks like (can you remember?).
She tells us about the sounds Tigger makes (can you remember?).
She tells us what Tigger smells of (can you remember?).
She tells us what Joe feels when he picks Tigger up or when Tigger comes to him (can you remember?).
And, in the café, taste suddenly becomes important (can you remember?).

This use of all five senses makes the story better because we too can experience it not just with our minds but also with our senses. Very often when we write stories or poems, we write about what happens and what we can see. If we also use sounds, smells, feelings and tastes, our writing will be much better, much more alive.

Clever Ideas That You Can Use Too

1 Using very short sentences and paragraphs for effect

2 Creating a character through the way they speak

3 Using all five senses

4 Deliberate repetition for effect

5 Connecting a taste with a powerful emotion

Four Ideas For Your Own Writing

Idea 1

Joe says, "A lot of folk think that cats are no as good as dogs; they don't dae tricks and they're kind of girlie pets...". What do you think about dogs versus cats as pets? Write about your experiences of dogs or cats and say what you like or dislike about each of them.

Idea 2

This story is not finished. Write what happens next. Think about whether you want to make the ending sad or happy. Can you come up with an ending which could be good for everyone – Joe, Danny and Tigger?

Idea 3

The arrival of a younger brother or sister changes everything. Write about the changes in your life, with the arrival of your little brother or sister. If you don't have a little brother or sister, write about how you feel about this – the good things and the bad things.

Idea 4

Danny suffers from an allergy. See if you can write a story about someone who has an extremely unusual allergy to something. Decide what the thing is and try to think of unusual ways in which the allergy could affect them. You might want to write it from your own point of view and create an allergy which could be the perfect excuse to stop you doing something you hate doing anyway! (Some pupils like to think they're allergic to homework...)

Picture 4

Use this picture to inspire you to write a story or a poem or a memory or a hope.

You can write about it in whatever way you wish, but it might help you to think about the following 8 questions. (There are no wrong answers...)

1   What does this seem to be?

2   What else might it be?

3   Who or what might be connected to this?

4   Where might it be?

5   When?

6   Who or what else might be involved?

7   What could happen next?

8   What sounds, smells or feelings could there be?

Chapter 15

Easter Eggs

Easter Eggs

My sister
brought her budgies home
for Easter

one green, one blue,
beaks sharper than
they looked,

quick little things.
I only pulled the door
a single inch –

a single inch
was all it took. No budgies left.
The door blew open

(yes, the wide back door).
Those budgies flew right up into the sky,
into the sharp, cool blue. I

called. They didn't listen;
left behind blue feathers, and green down
and husks of millet.

I knew my sister wouldn't like it.
That's why I've left these chocolate eggs
propped up in the cage...

Anne MacLeod

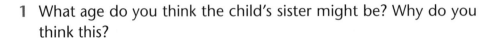

Questions

1   What age do you think the child's sister might be? Why do you think this?

2   What age do you think the child is? Why?

3   How do you think the little girl knew that their beaks are "sharper than they looked"?

4   Why do you think she opened the cage?

5   Do you believe her when she says it was only "a single inch"? Why?

6   Anne uses the word "sharp" both for the sky and for their beaks. We can understand how a sharp beak might hurt us with a peck, but in what way could the sky be "hurting" the child?

7   What does "cool" tell you about how the sky might be feeling?

8   Why do you think Anne uses the word "listen" instead of "hear"? What is the difference between listening to someone and hearing someone?

9   Why is the *sound* of the word "listen" better here than "hear"? (Read the sixth verse aloud and think about rhyme (p 36) and the way she is using "L" sounds.)

10   A husk means an empty case from which a seed has gone. Why is this a clever word to use here? (What else is now empty too?)

11   Why does the child choose to leave the chocolate eggs? Try to think of at least two reasons.

12   This poem happens at Easter time. Anne mentions husks and the birdcage is now empty too. What was also found to be empty on the first Easter Monday nearly 2000 years ago?

13   Do you know, or can you find out, what was also said to be left behind? How does this connect with what else is left behind in the cage?

→

Questions continued

14 Why do we have a tradition of rolling eggs at Easter time? What does the egg *symbolise*, that is, what does it stand for?

A Closer Look at Anne MacLeod's Writing Skills

Using line breaks dramatically

Poets take new lines for several reasons. For example, if you are writing verse with a regular rhythm like a limerick (p 127), then the rhythm will determine the line breaks. If you are writing free verse, without a regular rhythm or rhyme scheme, the line breaks are determined by the information in each line.

If you look at the first verse of Anne's poem, you will see three lines containing three pieces of important information for the poem.

If you look at the end of verse three and the start of verse four, you will see that Anne is using repetition, line break and verse break to balance the time *before* and the time *after* the escape of the birds.

If you look at the end of verse five, you will see an even more dramatic line break. Ann has split a two-word sentence ("I... called") across two verses. Because we would naturally pause at the end of the verse, this line-break creates the feeling of distance and time, of the child sending a call a long way up after the birds.

Anne is using a line break to make the information in the following line more surprising than it would be if it were in the same line. You can also see George Mackay Brown doing this at the end of the first line of his poem, "Island School" (p 143).

Next time you are writing a poem, look out for opportunities for dramatic line breaks. You can't use them all the time because then they would lose their impact, but if you use them occasionally, your poems will be better.

Playing with the sound of words

Although Anne's poem doesn't have a regular rhythm or rhyme, she has still used the sound of words to create patterns. For example, in verse one, she half-rhymes "sister... Easter". In verse two, she half-rhymes "green... beaks" and "blue... looked".

Read verse three aloud and count how many times Anne uses the "i" sound.

You can also find another "oo" rhyme in verse three, in the word "pulled". Anne could have used the word "opened" which would have had the same meaning, but the *sound* of the word wouldn't have connected with the poem so well.

If you look at verse three again, you will see that Anne is also using "l" sounds to capture the light, slightness of the little birds.

Read the rest of the poem aloud yourself, listening for rhymes or half-rhymes.

You can also hear Anne repeating sounds in the second last verse. Read this verse aloud again and listen for Anne's use of the sounds "l... f... s...". Think about whether these sounds are hard or soft and see if you can work out what feeling Anne is trying to give us.

Using poetic logic

Logic is when one thing inevitably leads to another. For example, if you go out in the rain, it is logical that you will get wet. Logic makes sense. Another example: if you drop a china mug on a stone floor, it will almost certainly break. And another: if you drop a metal spoon on the same floor, it will almost certainly *not* break. These are all logical consequences: they make sense in our world.

Writers like exploring other worlds. Writers can twist logic in a poetic way so that something *almost* makes sense. For example, it is logical that more budgies could hatch out of eggs, if they were the right kind of eggs and were kept warm.

However, chocolate eggs will never hatch into budgies. That would be illogical: it doesn't make sense. Chocolate eggs won't hatch into chocolate birds either, but by allowing ourselves to pretend that in a slightly different world they just might hatch into chocolate birds, we can use a poetic logic in order to be creative.

If we push the idea further, perhaps a chocolate bunny could sit on the chocolate eggs until they hatch into... flying rabbits?

By deliberately not making *complete* sense, we can come up with fantastic ideas to use in either poems or stories. Next time you find yourself saying, "But that couldn't possibly happen...", explore the idea and see where poetic logic takes you.

Working with two levels of meaning and symbols

You can read this poem on one level as a poem about two budgies that escape.

However, the use of Easter and Easter eggs makes the poem work on a second, deeper level. An Easter egg symbolises the big heavy stone that sealed the entrance to the cave which was the sepulchre where the body of Jesus was laid to rest after he had been crucified. Rolling an Easter egg symbolises the rolling away of the stone.

In the poem, the budgies fly up towards heaven and leave an empty cage behind. This can be seen as symbolising Jesus rising up from the dead. The feathers the birds leave behind can be seen as symbolising the shroud left behind in the empty cave. Angels also have wings like birds.

So, instead of this poem only being about two pet birds escaping, it can also be read as a religious poem about the resurrection.

Making a piece of writing work on two levels like this is a challenge. You might find an idea you are working on suddenly offers you a second level. If so, see if you can develop it. However, this is quite an advanced writing skill, so don't worry if your writing doesn't have a second level of meaning.

Clever Ideas That You Can Use Too

1   Using line breaks dramatically

2   Playing with the sound of words

3   Using poetic logic

4   Working with two levels of meaning

Four Ideas For Your Own Writing

Idea 1

See if you can write a poem about losing or breaking something that belongs to someone else. Make notes about what it might be, how you lose or break it, what you do to try to make things better.

When you've made your notes and are ready to draft your poem, try to use at least one dramatic line break.

Try to be aware of the sound of the words you use.

You might have some fun with poetic logic, if you let your imagination flow freely.

Idea 2

This poem ends before the big sister discovers that her pets have been allowed to escape. Write what happens next, when she finds out. You can write either a poem or a story. Try to use some dialogue if you are writing a story.

Idea 3

Write the story of what happens to the budgies. We last see them flying up into the sky. Will they be able to survive? Will somebody save them? Will they come back again on their own? Will someone else return them? What are their names? See what adventures you can write for the green and blue budgies.

Idea 4

What does Easter mean to you? Describe the three best things about your Easter.

Links between "Tigger" and "Easter Eggs"

Please make sure you have read both this story and this poem before you read any further.

There are quite a lot of similarities between "Tigger" and "Easter Eggs".

Both pieces of writing have the same subject: both are about separation from pets. In "Tigger", separation is not what Joe wants at all, because he loves his cat so much. In "Easter Eggs", the separation is a mistake, an accident not meant to happen. The little girl doesn't care about the birds: instead, she is worried that her big sister will be angry with her.

In "Tigger", it is the wee brother's suffering that means the cat may have to go. In "Easter Eggs", it is because the big sister has brought her budgies home, and because the little girl is fascinated by them, that they escape.

Both pieces of writing involve suffering. How many characters are, or will be, suffering in "Tigger"? List them and say how and why they are, or will be, suffering.

How many characters are, or will be, suffering in "Easter Eggs"? List them and say how and why they are, or will be, suffering.

Both "Tigger" and "Easter Eggs" have unfinished endings. Joe is uncertain, torn between Danny's suffering and his love for his cat. He hopes that keeping Tigger in the shed will be enough, but he knows in his heart that it won't be. In "Easter Eggs", there is more to come after the end of the poem. What does the wee girl hope might be enough? Do you think it will be?

When you look at these two pieces of writing this way, you can see the importance of conflict (p 44) and relationships and feelings between people and other creatures too.

If we think about writing skills, you can see that both writers use very short sentences for the most shocking statements. Anne Donovan uses one whole paragraph for one short sentence:

> "And now Mum wants me tae get rid of him."

Anne MacLeod's shocking sentence is even shorter:

> "No budgies left."

If you remember how powerful a short sentence can be for really shocking statements, then you too can use different lengths of sentences to make your writing more effective.

There are also some big differences between "Tigger" and "Easter Eggs".

As we have noted, Joe has a deep love and affection for Tigger, but the budgies don't even have names and the child doesn't love them.

In "Tigger", Joe has a horrible decision to make, in which he really has little choice: he is being asked to choose between a cat and his little brother. In "Easter Eggs", there are no decisions, only the consequences to be faced of having let the budgies go.

In "Tigger", because it is a story and is much longer than a poem, the characters are more clearly and deeply drawn, which means we can sympathise more with Joe's plight. In "Easter Eggs", the poem is short and Anne MacLeod is also playing with sounds and rhyme and verse pattern. She has another layer of Christian symbolism too. Her poem is not trying to make us care but to show us a pattern with words and sounds and events.

How well do you feel you know Joe and Tigger?

How well do you feel you know the little girl in "Easter Eggs"?

Which child do you care about more? Why?

Usually it is easier to create rounded characters in stories because we have so many more words to use. But if you want to play with patterns of sounds and meaning and rhyme, then poetry is better for that.

Before you choose whether to write a poem or a story, it helps if you decide the purpose of your piece of writing, that is, why you are writing it and what you want your readers to find in it.

Picture 5

Use this picture to inspire you to write a story or a poem or a memory or a hope.

You can write about it in whatever way you wish, but it might help you to think about the following 8 questions. (There are no wrong answers…)

1 What does this seem to be?

2 What else might it be?

3 Who or what might be connected to this?

4 Where might it be?

5 When?

6 Who or what else might be involved?

7 What could happen next?

8 What sounds, smells or feelings could there be?

Chapter 16

Limericks

Limericks are good fun. They are poems with a strong pattern of rhythm (p 32) and rhyme (p 36). Limericks are named after a place in Ireland called Limerick, and it was Edward Lear, the nineteenth-century Irish writer, who created many rhymes with this pattern.

They are often about unusual people. Here are four limericks for you:

There was a young man from Devizes
Whose ears were two different sizes
The one that was small
Was no use at all
But the larger one won several prizes.

There was a wee man from Darjeeling
Who boarded a bus bound for Ealing
The sign at the door
Said "Don't spit on the floor!"
So he stood up and spat on the ceiling.

A careless explorer called Blake
Fell into a tropical lake.
A fat alligator
A short while later
Said, "Nice, but I still prefer cake."

> The fabulous wizard of Oz
> Retired from business because
> What with up-to-date science
> For most of his clients
> He wasn't the wizard he was.

Maybe you know some other limericks you can share with the rest of the class?

A Closer Look at Skills for Writing Limericks

Here are some questions to help you to work out what the rules are for writing limericks.

Questions

1. How many lines does each limerick have?

2. How many different rhyme sounds?

3. What is the rhyming scheme? (p 37)

4. How many stressed syllables are there in each line? (p 33)

You should have worked out that a limerick has: five lines; two different rhyme sounds in an aabba rhyming scheme; lines 1, 2 and 5 have three stresses each; and lines 3 and 4 have two stresses each.

⌣　/　⌣　⌣　/　⌣　⌣　/　⌣
There **was** a young **man** from Dev**iz**es　　　　　a

　⌣　/　⌣　/　⌣　⌣　/　⌣
Whose **ears** were **two** different **siz**es　　　　　a

　⌣　/　⌣　⌣　/
The **one** that was **small**　　　　　b

　⌣　/　⌣　⌣　/
Was **no** use at **all**　　　　　b

⌣　⌣　/　⌣　⌣　/　⌣　⌣　/　⌣
But the **larg**er one **won** several **priz**es.　　　　　a

However, a limerick is really a four-line poem where the third line is divided into two lines to emphasise the rhyme that would otherwise be hidden in the middle of the line. It also has four beats in every line, although the last beat is silent in three of them:

ᵕ / ᵕ ᵕ / ᵕ ᵕ / ᵕ   /
There **was** a young **man** from De**viz**es   a

ᵕ   / ᵕ / ᵕ ᵕ / ᵕ   /
Whose **ears** were **two** different **siz**es   a

ᵕ / ᵕ ᵕ / ᵕ / ᵕ ᵕ /
The **one** that was **small** was **no** use at **all**   b/b

ᵕ ᵕ / ᵕ ᵕ / ᵕ ᵕ / ᵕ /
But the **larg**er one **won** several **priz**es.   a

If you know the tune to the nursery rhyme "Hickory Dickory Dock", you can check any limerick for correct rhythm and rhyme by singing it to this tune and clapping your hands in time to the stressed beats. This is because "Hickory Dickory Dock" is also in the form of a limerick, complete with the rests and the twin rhymes in the third line.

/ ˇ ˇ   / ˇ ˇ   /   /

Hickory **Dick**ory **Dock**   a

ˇ   /   ˇ /   ˇ /   /

The **mouse** ran **up** the **clock**   a

ˇ   /   ˇ /   ˇ /   ˇ /

The **clock** struck **one**, the **mouse** ran **down**   b/b

/ ˇ ˇ   / ˇ ˇ   /   /

Hickory **Dick**ory **Dock**   a

Now you can see how regular a pattern a limerick really has hiding behind it.

Here are some limericks for you where the writers have been having some real fun with words. Some are adding extra rhymes, or playing with pronunciation, or, in the last one, deliberately upsetting the rhythm.

> There was a young lady from Ryde
> Who ate some green apples and died,
> The apples fermented
> Inside the lamented
> And made cider inside her inside.

> There was a young damsel named Menzies
> Who asked, "Do you know what this thenzies?"
> Her aunt, with a gasp
> Replied, "It's a wasp
> And you're holding the end where the stenzies."

(To understand this limerick, you need to use the Scottish pronunciation of Menzies which sounds like "Ming-is". The anonymous writer has also used what looks like a perfect rhyme on the page with "gasp/wasp". This is called a visual rhyme,

because it *looks* perfect, but it becomes a half-rhyme
(p 39) when we say the words out loud "gasp/wosp".)

A daring young man from Milngavie
Had a burning ambition to flavie
So one day in the rain
He went up in a plane
And vanished when havie in the skavie.

(This limerick, written by Nick Larkin, again plays on
pronunciation. You need to know that the place name,
Milngavie, is pronounced "Mull-guy".)

A young man called Cholmondeley Colquhoun
Kept as a pet a babolquhoun
His mother said: "Cholmondeley,
D'you think it is colmondeley
To feed your babolquhoun with a spolquhoun?"

(To enjoy this one, you need to know how we pronounce both
Cholmondeley and Colquhoun!)

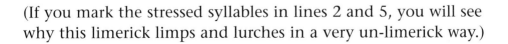

There was a young man from Japan
Whose limericks would never scan
He tried and he tried
But always he cried
"I want to make the last line as long as I possibly can!"

(If you mark the stressed syllables in lines 2 and 5, you will see
why this limerick limps and lurches in a very un-limerick way.)

Clever Ideas That You Can Use Too

1   Using rhythm

2   Using rhyme

3   Making up strange people and events

Using These Skills To Write Your Own Limericks

It may seem obvious, but start with a first line. Try several first lines and check that you can find at least two more rhymes for the last word before you go any further.

For example:

There was a young lady in blue / shoe / true / flew / flu / new / Sioux / Sue / drew…

Or

There was a young man from Dundee / see / flee / three / bee / tree / me…

Or

There was an old woman called Meg / peg / leg / egg / beg…

Or

There was an old man in a boat / goat / oat / stoat / throat…

Or

There was a wee pigeon from France / dance / chance / prance / glance / trance…

Use any of these first lines if you want and see where they take you. If you prefer, make up your own first line.

If you want to find rhyme words, work your way through the alphabet testing each letter with the rhyme sound: at… bat… cat… fat… hat… mat… gnat… pat… rat… sat… vat…

You can also get rhyming dictionaries where, instead of being given the meaning of the word, you are given words that rhyme with it. Like a thesaurus, which gives you other words with the same meaning, a rhyming dictionary can also give you lots of unexpected ideas. If your school doesn't have one, you could ask the librarian if they could get one.

Some sounds have more rhymes than others. Can you find a rhyme for orange?

Once you've got your first line, and you know you can find more rhymes for it, your second line and the following lines should come quite easily. Don't settle for your first ideas because often your later ideas will be better. Let your ideas run as wildly as you like and see where your limericks take you. Have fun!

Picture 6

Use this picture to inspire you to write a story or a poem or a memory or a hope.

You can write about it in whatever way you wish, but it might help you to think about the following 8 questions. (There are no wrong answers…)

1   What does this seem to be?

2   What else might it be?

3   Who or what might be connected to this?

4   Where might it be?

5   When?

6   Who or what else might be involved?

7   What could happen next?

8   What sounds, smells or feelings could there be?

Chapter 17

Zoo

Zoo

The children were always good during the month of August, especially when it began to get near the twenty-third. It was on this day that the great silver spaceship carrying Professor Hugo's Interplanetary Zoo settled down for its annual six-hour visit to the Chicago area.

Before daybreak, the crowds would form, long lines of children and adults both, each one clutching his or her dollar, and waiting with wonderment to see what race of strange creatures the Professor had brought this year.

In the past, they had sometimes been treated to three-legged creatures from Venus, or tall, thin men from Mars, or even snake-like horrors from somewhere more distant. This year, as the great round ship settled slowly to earth in the huge tri-city parking area just outside of Chicago, they watched with awe as the sides slowly slid up to reveal the familiar barred cages. In them were some wild breed of nightmare – small, horse-like animals that moved with quick, jerking motions and constantly chattered in a high-pitched tongue. The citizens of Earth clustered around as Professor Hugo's crew quickly collected the waiting dollars, and soon the good Professor himself made an appearance, wearing his many-coloured rainbow cape and top hat.

"Peoples of Earth," he called into his microphone.

The crowd's noise died down and he continued.

"Peoples of Earth, this year you see a real treat for your single dollar – the little-known horse-spider people of Kaan – brought to you across a million miles of space at great expense. Gather around, see them, study them, listen to them, tell your friends about them: but hurry! My ship can remain here only six hours!"

And the crowds slowly filed by, at once horrified and fascinated by these strange creatures that looked like horses but ran up the walls of their cages like spiders.

"This is certainly worth a dollar," one man remarked, hurrying away. "I'm going home to get the wife."

All day long it went like that, until ten thousand people had filed by the barred cages set into the side of the spaceship. Then, as the six-hour limit ran out, Professor Hugo once more took microphone in hand.

"We must go now, but we will return next year on this date. And if you enjoyed our Zoo this year, phone your friends in other cities about it. We will land in New York tomorrow, and next week on to London, Paris, Rome, Hong Kong, and Tokyo. Then on to other worlds!"

He waved farewell to them, and as the ship rose from the ground the Earth peoples agreed that this had been the very best Zoo yet...

Some two months and three planets later, the silver ship of Professor Hugo settled at last onto the familiar, jagged rocks of Kaan, and the queer horse-spider creatures filed quickly out of their cages. Professor Hugo was there to say a few parting words, and then they scurried away in a hundred different directions, seeking their homes among the rocks.

In one, the she-creature was happy to see the return of her mate and offspring: she babbled a greeting in the strange tongue and hurried to embrace them.

"It was a long time you were gone. Was it good?"

And the he-creature nodded.

"The little one enjoyed it especially. We visited eight worlds and saw many things."

The little one ran up the wall of the cave.

"On the place called Earth it was the best. The creatures there wear garments over their skins, and they walk on two legs."

"But isn't it dangerous?" asked the she-creature.

"No," her mate answered. "There are bars to protect us from them. We remain right in the ship. Next time you must come with us. It is well worth the nineteen commocs it costs."

And the little one nodded. "It was the very best Zoo ever…"

Edward D. Hoch

Questions

1 Which two words in the first paragraph tell you this is science fiction?

2 Which one word in the first paragraph tells you that Professor Hugo brings his zoo every year?

3 Edward has changed the meaning of "nightmare". What do we normally understand by the word and what has he chosen to make it mean instead?

4 Why do you think people were both horrified and fascinated by the horse-spiders?

Questions continued

5 The story could finish at the first ellipsis (the three dots), as the spaceship leaves Chicago. Why does the second part of the story make it better?

6 What changes are there in the second part of the story? Think about setting (p 49), point of view (p 39) and how the characters of the horse-spiders are developed.

7 What two things does the horse-spider he-creature find so strange about Earth people?

8 How does Edward manage to surprise us with his ending – which one sentence near the end turns around completely the idea of "zoo"?

9 What pattern do you see in both punctuation and words at the end of each section?

10 What kind of person is Professor Hugo and what makes him such a good businessman?

A Closer Look at Edward D. Hoch's Writing Skills

Looking and wondering

Looking and wondering may not seem like writing skills, but they are an important part of inspiration. Edward will have gone to a zoo and looked at the animals in their cages. He would have taken time to think about them and to wonder exactly whom the bars were there to protect. We assume the bars are there to protect us from the animals, but, as writers, we can get good ideas by turning assumptions on their heads and then following them.

Edward, instead of just going home for his tea and forgetting about it, would have thought about how he could use this in a story and about what characters he might need to create.

He might have tried several ideas before he developed this one. You too will find that you can come up with better ideas if you take time to look at and wonder about whatever you see around you.

Using a pattern and repetition

You will have noticed that the story is in two parts. Each of them starts with the spaceship landing and each of them ends with the same phrase and similar punctuation. This similarity helps to emphasise how different things are in the second part of the story and makes the ending even more effective.

You too can write a two-part story where things are very different in the second part. If you deliberately use similar words or situations, particularly at the beginning or the ending of your parts, your story will work better.

Creating a twist ending

Edward has created a clever twist ending here where we realise that the horse-spiders think they have *been to* a zoo, and that the humans don't realise that they were *in* a zoo. We, the readers, feel superior because we also know that neither the humans nor the horse-spiders realise how Professor Hugo has made money from them both.

If you want to create a twist ending, you need to work out what it's going to be before you start writing your story. Then you lead your reader along one path (Earth people going to Interplanetary Zoo) before twisting this idea at the end (horse-spiders going to Earth Zoo). You can also find a good twist ending in Maureen Sullivan's short story, "An Eye for an Eye" (p 171).

Inventing people and creatures

Edward has created an imaginary creature, the "horse-spider", by thinking about two creatures that are very different and combining them. This is like creating a character by using two different people you know. So, for example, if you know someone who really likes eating beetroot and who is always spilling their food, and you know someone else who always wears perfectly clean, white clothes, then you can roll them into one character, dressed in beetroot-stained, white clothes, who may or may not care about the state of their clothes. This could be the starting point of an interesting story.

Imaginary creatures can be half-human or they can be completely strange. Other people have created imaginary creatures already. Do you know what a mermaid is?
Do you know what a centaur is? Do you know what a harpy is? See if you can find out, if you don't already know. Can you think of any other half-human creatures? We will return to the creation of strange creatures in the section on writing ideas.

Clever Ideas That You Can Use Too

1 Looking and wondering

2 Using a pattern and repetition

3 Creating a twist ending

4 Inventing people and creatures

Four Ideas For Your Own Writing

Idea 1

Edward has created the "horse-spider" by crossing the idea of a horse with a spider – it behaves like both creatures. Write about what happens when you bring a young horse-spider home as a pet. You might like to add some more details about its appearance, its behaviour and the sounds that it makes and the way that it smells.

Idea 2

Professor Hugo brings his zoo every year. We know a little about some of the creatures he has brought in previous years (see paragraph 3 of the story). Write an article for your local paper about the creatures he will be bringing next time. Create them by crossing two very different kinds of creatures, like the horse-spider. Decide how they behave, what they eat, what they look like and what noises they make.

Design a poster to advertise this next visit from the Interplanetary Zoo.

You might find a story idea forming in your head as you create your strange creatures. Please let yourself write it, if you do.

Idea 3

Zoos used to be very popular. Write about what you think of zoos. If you have visited one, write about what you felt was good or bad about it. If you have never visited a zoo, write about what you think is good or bad about keeping creatures in zoos. Why do you think that zoos might be less popular now?

Idea 4

Edward uses several unusual terms (she-creature, he-creature and commocs) in the second part of the story which is set on Kaan.

Imagine you too have just returned from visiting another world. Write your diary entry for the day when you came under threat and had to think quickly to save your life. Create your own words for some of the creatures or objects in this other world.

Picture 7

Use this picture to inspire you to write a story or a poem or a memory or a hope.

You can write about it in whatever way you wish, but it might help you to think about the following 8 questions. (There are no wrong answers...)

1 What does this seem to be?

2 What else might it be?

3 Who or what might be connected to this?

4 Where might it be?

5 When?

6 Who or what else might be involved?

7 What could happen next?

8 What sounds, smells or feelings could there be?

Island School

A boy leaves a small house
  Of sea light. He leaves
    The sea smells, creel
    And limpet and cod.

The boy walks between steep
  Stone houses, echoing
    Gull cries, the all-around
    Choirs of the sea,

Ship noises, shop noises, clamours
  Of bellman and milkcart.
    The boy comes at last
    To a tower with a tall desk

And a globe and a blackboard
  And a stern chalk-
    smelling lady. A bell
    Nods and summons.

A girl comes, cornlight
  In the eyes, smelling
    Of peat and cows
    And the rich midden.

Running she comes, late,
  Reeling in under the last
    Bronze brimmings. She sits
    Among twenty whispers.

George Mackay Brown

Questions

1 The first line of this poem is simple, "A boy leaves a small house…". The next three words George uses, "…of sea light", change everything. If he'd said a small house of brick or stone or wood, we would understand what he meant. What do you think he means by "a small house / of sea light"?

2 Where must the boy be going, if he also leaves behind the smells of the sea?

3 George uses the word "steep" to describe the stone houses. We know what a steep hill is, or a steep roof, but what do you think he means by "steep stone houses"?

4 List the different sounds in verses two and three that the boy hears on his way to school.

Questions continued

5   Do you think his school is really a tower? Why might it seem like a tower to him?

6   George mentions four things in the classroom: a tall desk, a globe, a blackboard and a stern chalk-smelling lady. Which of these can you find in your classroom today? What would you say are the four things in your classroom that make it most like a school?

7   When do you think this poem is set? Why?

8   How do you think the teacher wanted her pupils to feel about her? How do you know this?

9   Why do you think George says the school bell "nods and summons" instead of simply "rings"?

10 In the second last verse, George again uses light and smells. What do you think the girl's eyes look like and where do you think the girl lives?

11 George could simply have said the girl was late but he says she comes "running" and "reeling in". Can you explain what "reeling" adds to the way she is moving?

12 What do you think the "last bronze brimmings" might be? (The school bell is made of a metal called bronze.)

13 The poem has been filled with the outside sounds, smells and movements of the island world. Why do you think it ends so quietly? What do you think the pupils might be whispering?

14 How do you think the pupils feel about their teacher? Why do you think this?

15 Do you think George thinks school is a good place or not? Why?

A Closer Look at George Mackay Brown's Writing Skills

Using words in unexpected ways

George uses words in unexpected ways. When he writes about "a house of sea light... steep stone houses... cornlight in the eyes... bronze brimmings... twenty whispers..." he is pushing language. He is trying to make us think about what it could mean. He is also trying to give us enough clues to get close to understanding what he means.

Using a pattern

George first describes the boy's journey to school, then the girl's journey to school, then the change in their behaviour when they get there. He uses light and smell and sound to help us experience it.

Playing with the sound of words

George enjoys playing with sounds, playing with the music of words. Look again at the first verse. Count how many times he uses the "ee" sound, how many times he uses an "l" sound and how many times he uses an "s" sound.

This is deliberate. Read the verse again, slowly, aloud, and see if you can feel what mood he is trying to create by repeating these sounds.

How many times does he use "b" or "r" in this first verse?

How many times does he use "b" or "r" in the first three lines of the last verse?

How many times does he use "s" or "sh" in the last sentence?

Read this last verse again, slowly, aloud. Listen to how the "b" and "r" sounds connect to the rushing movements, and then to how the "s" and "sh" sounds connect to the almost-silence of the whispering children.

George has deliberately chosen words for their sound as well as for their meaning.

Clever Ideas That You Can Use Too

1   Using words in unexpected ways

2   Using a pattern

3   Playing with the sound of words

Four Ideas For Your Own Writing

Idea 1

Write a poem about two children who have very different journeys to school. You can make one child late if you wish.

Make notes about the sounds, lights and smells they leave at home and find on the way to school. Think about the sounds of the words that you are using. Soft letters include "l... m... n... s...". Harder letters include "b... d... k... p... r... t...".

You can create "lights" in the same way as George does, by putting an unexpected word in front of it. For example, "dance light... black light... slow light..." which suggest something to your reader, rather than tell them exactly. You can create other unexpected ideas by putting together any two words that you would not normally find together.

Describe how the two children are moving to school. Are they on foot, cycling, being driven, taking the bus, or something else?

Describe also how their behaviour changes, once they get into the classroom.

Idea 2

It is likely that this island school has only one teacher and that the total number of pupils, of all ages, is only 21. (George belonged to the Orkney Islands, which are just off the north coast of Scotland.) Write about what you think would be the good and bad things about going to either a small school on an island, or a big school in a city.

147

Idea 3

Write about the area where your school is situated. Write about how big your school is and what the three best and three worst things about its location are.

Idea 4

George has written a poem about people who fish or farm. Do they need watches or bells? What "clocks" do they live by? Write about how much your life depends on knowing the time. How much could you live by the sun instead?

Finally, here are six questions for you to think about and discuss.

1 Do you think the Island School pupils would be happier outside?

2 What do you think they need to learn in order to make a living on their island? Do you think they will be getting taught this at school?

3 What do you think pupils actually want to learn?

4 How much of what you are learning at school do you actually want to learn?

5 What would you like to learn that you are not getting at school?

6 What do you think is the best way to help young people to learn about life? From a computer? In schools? In the family? With other people? Somewhere else?

Picture 8

Use this picture to inspire you to write a story or a poem or a memory or a hope.

You can write about it in whatever way you wish, but it might help you to think about the following 8 questions. (There are no wrong answers...)

1   What does this seem to be?
2   What else might it be?
3   Who or what might be connected to this?
4   Where might it be?
5   When?
6   Who or what else might be involved?
7   What could happen next?
8   What sounds, smells or feelings could there be?

Chapter 19

Clydesdale

Things you might need to know before reading "Clydesdale"

This is one of a series of four poems that Edwin Morgan has written about horses. The Clydesdale horse is the gentle giant of the horse world, around eight feet tall to the tips of its ears. In the late nineteenth century and well into the twentieth century, they were used in farming throughout Scotland to pull the plough. They were also used, in the towns and the cities, to pull heavy carts, laden with anything from grain to stone: they would pull whatever we now load onto lorries.

We used Clydesdale horses to do heavy work here in the same way as elephants were (and still are) used in the timber industry in Asia.

Clydesdale horses are magnificent, strong animals with long manes, long tails and lots of long silky hair on their ankles which flows around their huge hooves when they walk. This hair on each ankle is called a fetlock, perhaps from "foot-lock" which suggests locks of hair on their feet. (We also have the word "forelock", which means a lock of hair on our forehead.)

Today, Clydesdale horses can be seen, and perhaps ridden, in farm parks: Glasgow, Aberdeen and Dundee City Councils all keep Clydesdale horses. They can also be seen advertising whisky distilleries or breweries by pulling shiny carts laden with polished barrels of whisky or beer, the way they used to do when they were working in the old days. Lothian and Borders Police have working Clydesdale horses in their mounted section and Clydesdale horses, beautifully groomed and decorated, may sometimes be seen drawing a coach to a wedding. This sculpture of a Clydesdale horse can be seen from the M8 motorway in Glasgow.

They are called Clydesdale horses because they were bred in Lanarkshire and the old name for Lanarkshire was Clydesdale, where the River Clyde has its source.

Now, read the poem on the next page, slowly, aloud.

Clydesdale

go
    fetlocksnow
        go
          gullfurrow
            go

go
    brassglow
        go
          sweatflow
            go

go
    plodknow
        go
          clodshow
            go

go
    leatherbelow
        go
          potatothrow
            go

go
    growfellow
        go
          crowfollow
            go

go
    Balerno
        go
          Palermo
           whoa

Edwin Morgan

Questions

Read this poem again, slowly, aloud.

1   What do you think is happening?

2   This is an unusual poem with a clear pattern on the page. Describe this layout – how many verses can you see? How many lines in each verse? How many words in each line?

3   Can you see any more patterns or repetitions?

4   How has Edwin used rhyme? What do you notice about the very last rhyme?

A Closer Look at Edwin Morgan's Writing Skills

Using Kennings

With each of the bigger double-words, Edwin is summing up an aspect of the horses or the field that they are working in. For example, the first verse contains the double-words "fetlocksnow" and "gullfurrow". In normal English, Edwin is telling us that "the hair of the horses' fetlocks is as white as snow" and "there are seagulls flocking around the furrows".

Can you expand the double-words in the other five verses into sentences?

Now you will understand the clever way Edwin is squashing, or compressing, the ideas into double-words. This is something poets from northern Europe were doing centuries ago and the name for this compressed expression is a "kenning". This means a way of knowing, but differently, like a riddle. The Scots word for "know" is "ken": perhaps you've come across the song, "Dae ye ken John Peel?"

Ancient kennings, from Old English, for the sea include "swanroad… sailroad… whaleway… whaleroad…". Can you think of any other kennings for the sea?

Another kenning is "quicksilver" which means silver that appears to be "quick" or alive, and which is another word for mercury. Mercury is a silver metal that is liquid at room temperature and well below. It doesn't become solid until the temperature drops down to around –38° (both Farenheit and Centigrade). It is the silver liquid that we use in thermometers. On its own, a drop of mercury is like a very heavy, very slippery silver bead, so "alive" that it is almost impossible to hold it in your hand: if it drops onto floorboards, it shatters into dozens of tiny silver beads which bounce and scatter and vanish down the cracks. It's also very poisonous.

Sometimes kennings are used as nicknames for people who are skilled at, or perhaps very bad at, something. What do you think Thornfinn Skullsplitter or Erik Bloodaxe did for a living? (See if you can find out who they were, and when and where they lived.)

Can you think of any kenning nicknames for people you know? Try to be flattering rather than insulting, if you can!

Using an unusual layout

Edwin could have written his poem with every word against the left-hand margin, like this:

go
fetlocksnow
go
gullfurrow
go

Instead, he has chosen to spread it across the page. Why do you think he has done this? How has this improved the poem?

Clever Ideas That You Can Use Too

1   Using kennings
2   Using an unusual layout
3   Repeating the same word to create a rhythm
4   Using only one rhyme sound

Three Ideas For Your Own Writing

Idea 1

Let's see if we can come up with some kennings from the following sentence:

The hound, which is as black as night, chases the white rabbit.

Here are some possible kennings for the dog:
nighthound…blackhound…nightdog…jetdog (jet is a black gemstone and also has the idea of speed)…jetfur…soothound…

Here are some possible kennings for the rabbit:
snowrabbit…snowfur…snowbunny…arrowrabbit…rabbitfear…rabbitrun…

And for the whole sentence: rabbithound…rabbitchaser…rabbithunter…bunnyhunt…houndfood…dogfood…

There are no rights and wrongs here. Instead, we are playing with words and ideas to see where they might take us. Kennings suggest meanings, like riddles. They are the opposite of clear and obvious.

You don't have to use exactly the same words: you can also use words (like "snow" or "arrow") which are connected in some way.

Now see if you can come up with two or more kennings from each of the following three sentences:

A thrush is sitting singing in the cherry tree.

The stone wall crumbles and falls down.

The thorn on the white rose made her finger bleed.

Idea 2

Edwin has written his poem about two horses ploughing a field in which potatoes are being sown. He describes the horses, the land, their movements, their harnesses, the birds around them and their size.

Think of an animal or a person who is doing something repetitive and which finally stops (cycling... flying... swimming...?). Try to write 10 sentences each describing one detail. This might be a detail of colour, movement, smell, sound, taste, weather or setting.

Create kennings, as you did with Idea 1, from your descriptive sentences. Create as many kennings as you can.

Choose the 10 best ones.

If you want, try to think of one word (or one rhyme) that could be used all the way through, as Edwin has used "go (whoa)". Cycling could be push / push / push; flying could be beat / beat / beat or flap / flap / flap; swimming could be glide / glide / glide...

Arrange your poem on the page. You can follow Edwin's layout, or you can create your own pattern with words and spaces.

Idea 3

We no longer need to use horses to help us. Why not? Write about the changes and inventions that have replaced them. What are the advantages and disadvantages of the way our lives were in the time of horses, and the way our lives are now? (Think about how your life would be different without machinery, engines, electricity...)

Picture 9

Use this picture to inspire you to write a story or a poem or a memory or a hope.

You can write about it in whatever way you wish, but it might help you to think about the following 8 questions. (There are no wrong answers...)

1   What does this seem to be?

2   What else might it be?

3   Who or what might be connected to this?

4   Where might it be?

5   When?

6   Who or what else might be involved?

7   What could happen next?

8   What sounds, smells or feelings could there be?

Chapter 20

All That Glitters

Things you might need to know before reading "All That Glitters"

You may have heard of a proverb or saying, "All that glitters...". Perhaps you know the end of it too? We will return to this title at the end of the story and see how we can use proverbs for ideas.

There are perhaps three words in the story you might not know:

Possessed – if you are possessed by something, you are under its spell and it has control of your mind.

Obsessed – if you are obsessed with something, you can think of nothing else but that.

Languishing – if you are languishing somewhere, you are lying around, feeling fed up and neglected.

This story is set in a time when we used old money. 1/6 (one and six) means one shilling and sixpence. Although 1/6 would be worth less than 8p today, it had the same buying power then as three times your pocket money has now.

All That Glitters

It was all the angel's fault.

From the moment I saw her, I was possessed. She was a vision with rich golden wings and a beautiful dress; the first sight of her left me breathless. I had to have her.

Which was a big problem since I was only six years old and she was in a shop window proudly displaying a price tag of 1/6.

➜

I became obsessed with her. Of course I didn't know a big word like that then, but my every waking moment was filled with the angel.

At school, I could think of nothing but touching those golden wings, smoothing that lovely lace dress. After school, I'd lag behind the others as we approached Keenan's shop: I'd wait until they had all bought their penny caramels and were chewing down the road, then I'd press my face to the shop window and behold my angel in private and with a lump in my throat. At home, I'd picture her sitting in all her glory atop the Christmas tree.

Nothing seemed right in my life until I could have that angel. That night, I had no enthusiasm for the decorations Dad was putting up. As everyone stepped back to admire them, I hardly raised my eyes. There was no way they could look anything until my angel was presiding over them.

As Dad crowned the tree with the usual old battered star and Mum and my older brother and younger sister cheered, my depression deepened. I slipped quietly into the room and lay on my bed to think about my angel languishing in Keenan's shop window.

I had to have that angel. Then I had a terrible thought. Suppose... suppose someone had bought her already? Suppose she was gone from the window and was at this very moment sitting on top of someone else's tree? I closed my eyes. I couldn't bear to think about that. About someone else having a wonderfully happy life because they had my angel. There was no point in asking Mum and Dad. They always used the same old decorations every year. Like most parents they confused tradition with stinginess.

It was painful for me to think that only 1/6 separated me from pure happiness.

Then I had an idea. 1/6 was the price of my angel: it was a lot of money for me, but the figure also rang another bell in my head which could be the answer to my prayer.

It was the combined pocket monies of me, my brother and my sister. Suppose they were suddenly overcome with generosity...? Suppose they were to give me their sixpences...? Suppose I could persuade them to chip in and buy...?

My sister was no problem. She was only five years old and looked up to me the way little sisters do. I'd get her sixpence no problem. My brother was a different story for two reasons – he was older than me and he was a boy. He'd no sooner get his sixpence than it was spent on comics and mojos. He had no interest in anything with wings unless you could sit Captain Scarlett in it. I'd need to work on him.

I waited until the Friday when we came home from school. There was always a period of anticipation between then and when Dad came home with his pay packet and more importantly our pocket money.

I began by remarking to my brother about how rubbish our tree looked and then went on to describe the wonderful angel who would not only brighten up our tree, but our Christmas and indeed our lives.

I can't remember exactly what I said but by the time I'd finished I must have made that angel seem like the eighth wonder of the world, because he agreed to give me his sixpence the minute he got it.

Sure enough, Dad handed the sixpences out and immediately my brother and sister handed them over to me, their eyes shining with anticipation as I set out on my quest to Keenan's.

I could hardly bear to look in the window. But Hallelujah! She was still there. I stood for a moment savouring the knowledge that in a few seconds she would be mine – well ours... but really mine.

There was a queue in the shop, men coming home from work, in to buy their papers and cigarettes, and kids spending their pocket money on sweets. I waited anxiously, my heart beating hard. Then disaster, Mr. MacKenzie from the next close told Mrs. Keenan he was looking for something nice for his wife and asked about my angel. As Mrs. Keenan went to fetch it out of the window, I felt as though I was going to faint. I tried to get my mouth to work. I tried to shout, "That's mine!" but the words were heavy like treacle and oozed out my mouth in a muffled gooey mess which no one heard, except Mr. Keenan who asked if I was choking. In the meantime, Mr. MacKenzie had changed his mind and asked for a box of After Eights instead.

I breathed again.

Finally it was my turn. My voice was squeaky as I asked for the angel. I couldn't believe how straightforward it was: I asked for it, Mrs. Keenan went into the window for it, I handed over money, she popped my angel into a brown bag and gave me it. It was that simple. My angel was mine.

I hurried out of the shop just in case the Keenans suddenly remembered that the angel was for someone else, or that I hadn't given them the right money or something.

I carried it in my hand, my arm outstretched, and walked carefully down the road. My heart swelled with happiness. I felt very important, as though I were carrying the Baby Jesus himself.

My brother and sister were waiting in the hall when I got back. They held their breaths as they saw the bag. I handed it to my brother. Give him his place, he was the oldest. Besides I couldn't bear to open the bag in front of them in case my joy should overflow and they found out the kind of idiot I was. As my brother reached into the bag, I closed my eyes. I couldn't bear to see her in another's hand.

I listened for the gasps of amazement.

Instead, I heard my sister wail. I opened my eyes and saw my brother's horrified face.

"You spent our pocket money on THAT!"

He held her by the feet.

"I want my sixpence! I want a Dainty and Parma Violets!" my sister yelled. My brother was still looking at the angel the way he had looked at the dead rat Charlie Bubbles had found in the back last week.

I looked at her.

She was nothing more than a small baby doll with a piece of pink net wrapped around her middle. Her wings were made of cardboard stuck through her back with a large staple and half of the gold glitter still lay in the brown bag. She looked nothing like a majestic angel: she looked like a tacky doll dressed up for Hallowe'en.

Now, I had a serious situation on my hands. My brother and sister were demanding their sixpence back.

Dad came out to see what all the fuss was about. He heard the whole sorry story and laughed. He took the angel into the living room and stuck her on top of the tree, still laughing about something called fools and their money. My sister was still sobbing and my brother glowering at me, while Mum tried to diffuse the situation saying how beautiful the angel looked on the tree. She didn't. Mum or the angel. Later that night, Dad said he hoped we had all learned a lesson.

I don't think we did though.

Because every Christmas, even now as adults, my sister and brother hand me money and entrust me to buy our parents' Christmas presents. And as I rush through town in the sleet on Christmas Eve, I'm still trying to work out who the fool is – still, they've never again demanded their money back – yet!

Carolyn Mack

Questions

1 The little girl telling us this story says she was obsessed: that her "every waking moment was filled with the angel". Explain the three ways in which she was obsessed – during school, on the way home and at home.

2 How does the little girl hope the angel will change her life?

3 Can you explain the sentence "like most parents, they confused tradition with stinginess"? What is the little girl wishing they would do instead?

4 Why will it be easy for the little girl to get her sister's pocket money?

5 Why will her brother be less easy to persuade?

6 Why does she choose after school on Friday to try to get her brother and sister's pocket money?

7 How did she manage to persuade her brother to part with his pocket money?

8 As she is waiting to buy the angel, she says, "in a few seconds, she would be mine... well, ours... but really mine." Can you explain this?

9 How does her brother show his contempt for the angel in the way he holds her and looks at her?

10 Quote two phrases, from near the beginning of the story, that describe the angel before the little girl has bought her.

11 Quote three phrases that describe the angel, after she's bought her, when she finally looks closely at her.

12 Why has this change happened?

13 Why does their father find it so funny?

14 How does their mother react?

→

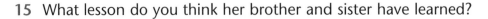

Questions continued

15 What lesson do you think her brother and sister have learned?

16 Their father laughs about something called "fools and their money". Do you know what the rest of the saying, "A fool and his money…" is? What lesson did their father hope they would learn?

17 At the very end, we come back to the present time. What final lesson do you think her brother and sister have learned?

18 Who would you say is the fool at the end, and why?

A Closer Look at Carolyn Mack's Writing Skills

Using conflict and turning points

If you're able to use them, turning points are very effective in a story. Carolyn uses them well here. Several times she leads us to expect one thing and then she turns around our expectations and takes the story in a different direction.

For example, this story could have a very simple structure: girl sees pretty angel, girl buys pretty angel, girl likes pretty angel. This would be a story without much conflict or action or strong feelings.

Instead, Carolyn creates complications and obstacles.

Girl sees what she thinks is a pretty angel and wants to buy it.

Problem 1 – she can't afford it.

Possible solution – get her brother and sister's pocket money.

Problem 2 – getting her brother's pocket money.

Solution – persuade him with dramatic exaggeration.

Having got the pocket money, problems 1 and 2 are solved, so she goes to buy the doll.

Problem 3 – conflict – Mr MacKenzie seems to want it for his wife.

Solution – Mr MacKenzie buys After Eights instead.

Girl buys doll.

Turning point – instead of loving it, her brother and sister hate it and instead of loving it herself, she realises how cheap it is.

Problem 4 – conflict – her brother and sister are upset and angry and want their money back.

Ending – instead of being happy because she now has what she wanted, they are all older and wiser. She has learned to look more closely at things and her brother and sister have learned neither to believe her exaggerations, nor to let her persuade them to part with their pocket money again.

Final turning point – her brother and sister now *choose* to give her money, to save them the bother of finding and buying their parents a Christmas present in bad weather on busy Christmas Eves. It's almost like revenge or punishment for what she did to them so many years ago.

When we break the story down like this, we can see how carefully Carolyn has planned it. She has deliberately stopped the story going smoothly by creating obstacles and problems, and several times she turns the story around completely when something we do not expect happens.

This story is a good example of how useful turning points and conflict can be.

Using strong feelings

Carolyn exaggerates feelings to make her story more effective. For example, if the little girl had just quite liked the angel it would have been much weaker. Instead, the little girl is completely obsessed and totally passionate about how much she wants this angel. Having created this excited character, Carolyn has fun in the shop when the little girl is so concerned that she tries to protest and the shopkeeper thinks that she is choking.

Carolyn also uses strong feelings when the little girl's brother and sister react to the tacky angel – her sister starts wailing, then gets angry and then starts sobbing, while her brother is disgusted and furious, and they both want their money back.

Using opposite feelings like this makes the story more entertaining and the characters more alive.

Describing something in two very different ways

Carolyn manages to describe the angel, through the little girl's eyes, in two very different ways. This is how Carolyn makes her character develop in the story, by having her change in the way that she sees things.

At the beginning, the angel seems perfect, beautiful and valuable. At the end, the angel is just a cheap and disappointing doll. What has changed is the way the little girl sees the angel. She has learnt to see more clearly, to look more closely, not to be deceived by appearances.

Using proverbs

The title of this story is the first half of the proverb "All that glitters isn't gold". A proverb is a saying which is trying to teach us something and perhaps warn us about mistakes we could make.

"All that glitters isn't gold" is warning us that not all shiny yellow things are as valuable as genuine gold. Can you think of any things that look like gold but that are much less valuable than real gold? If you look around you, you will probably see things that look like gold, or perhaps silver…

Carolyn also refers to another proverb at the end of the story, "A fool and his money are soon parted". This means that if you are stupid, it's easy to take your money, or anything valuable, from you. In this story, all three children were fools: the little girl was clever enough to take money from her brother and sister who were foolish enough to believe her, but she was foolish enough to let the "angel" in the shop window persuade her to part with their money.

Here are six more proverbs. Can you explain what they are trying to teach you?

1   Look before you leap.

2   A stitch in time saves nine.

3   Make hay while the sun shines.

4   Let sleeping dogs lie.

5   More haste less speed.

6   No smoke without fire.

Can you think of any other proverbs?

Proverbs can be good starting points for stories because they often suggest an action and also some conflict. For example, if we take "look before you leap", we have the action of someone jumping into something which might not turn out to be what they expected. This could become a story about a boy who thinks he is jumping on to the snow-covered roof of a garage when, instead, he goes crashing through a snow-covered greenhouse roof. If he had looked more carefully before he leapt, he might not have fallen.

Around this, we can build a story about why the boy was there in the first place and about what happened afterwards. We can create other characters – his friends, the owner of the greenhouse, his parents – and also create more action and conflict.

We could use the same proverb to create a very different story with different characters and different conflict. Proverbs can have lots of stories behind them and can be very useful if you're stuck for ideas.

Clever Ideas That You Can Use Too

1   Using conflict and turning points

2   Using strong feelings

3   Describing something in two very different ways

4   Using proverbs

Seven Ideas For Your Own Writing

Idea 1

Write a story about someone who is desperate to have something which seems impossibly far away from them and very difficult to get. Write about whether they manage to get it or not. Before you start, decide whether they will be happy or not with it, if they finally do get it.

Idea 2

Write about a time when you saved up for something and about how you felt when you finally got it. If you are saving up for something just now, you can write about that instead. Explain why you want it and how you think it will change your life.

Idea 3

Have you ever persuaded someone to do something because of your enthusiasm? Write about why they didn't want to do it, and how you managed to persuade them to do it.

Idea 4

Have you ever been persuaded to do something by someone else? Write about what it was, and how they managed to persuade you, and whether it was worth your while.

Idea 5

Research some more proverbs. Choose one as inspiration for a story.

Idea 6

Carolyn writes, when the little girl is trying to persuade her brother, "I can't remember exactly what I said, but by the time I'd finished, I must have made that angel seem like the eighth wonder of the world..."

There are seven ancient places that are known as The Seven Wonders of the World. Most of them disappeared long ago, but see if you can research what they were. Then see if you can think of a better eighth wonder of the world than the doll in the story. Write about why this place or object deserves to be the eighth wonder of the world.

Idea 7

Think about what might be the Seven Wonders of Scotland. List any wonderful natural places, or amazing buildings, or eye-catching statues or bridges, or strange big stones, or ancient remains or anything at all that you are familiar with, which could be one of the Seven Wonders of Scotland. You can do this in small groups, if you like, and use photographs and drawings too.

Picture 10

Use this picture to inspire you to write a story or a poem or a memory or a hope.

You can write about it in whatever way you wish, but it might help you to think about the following 8 questions. (There are no wrong answers...)

1   What does this seem to be?

2   What else might it be?

3   Who or what might be connected to this?

4   Where might it be?

5   When?

6   Who or what else might be involved?

7   What could happen next?

8   What sounds, smells or feelings could there be?

Chapter 21

An Eye for an Eye

One thing you might need to know before reading "An Eye for an Eye".

There is one word in this story you may not know – seg. A seg is a little stud of metal that men used to hammer into the heels and toe-tips on their shoes. Segs stopped the soles, which used to be made of leather, from wearing down too quickly. They also made a sharp clicking noise when you walked which made some men feel more important. (There is a song, written by Paul Simon, about a woman so rich that she has diamonds in the soles of her shoes...)

An Eye for an Eye

He wis a legend, so he wis: well, at least in our livin room.

Ma Uncle Pat. Ma Uncle Pat the Hat McVitie. He wis ma faither's big brother and he lived abroad. He hud tae: he wis oan the run.

Ah used tae say his name out loud. Ah loved sayin it.

"Ah'm Pat the Hat McVitie", Ah'd say, standin in front o the mirror in ma mither's bedroom. Ah'd stand as tall as Ah could, ma shoulders pulled back, legs wide apart, hands buried deep into ma pockets. Ah'd clear ma throat, lower ma voice and make ma eyes intay wee slits. Ma voice wis never as deep as Ah wid huv liked but Ah wisnae gonny let a wee thing like that stop me, after all, Ah wis the nephew o the Hat.

"You, ya slippery slug, c'mere!" Ah'd growl intae thin air, pushin my chin as far away fae ma body as Ah could. Ah tried to

→

look mean but sometimes deep doon Ah thought Ah looked a bit stupit. This worried me: maybe Ah wisnae related tae the Hat? Maybe Ah wisnae his real nephew? Maybe Ah wis adopted? Even if Ah wis, Ah still hid tae be prepared coz ye never know when ye might end up in a shootout wi the mob fae Cranhill and they wouldnae know Ah wis adopted. The chances of this happenin wurnae very high coz Ah wis only seven year auld but still, ye jist never really knew.

Ma faither wid wait till ma mither wis oot at the bingo before he wid tell me aw aboot ma Uncle Pat. He said it wis tae be jist between me and him – men's talk. Ah felt really special and proud tae be a McVitie and this stayed wi me for the rest o ma life. Ah looked forward tae these times, these stories aboot Uncle Pat, in fact Ah couldnae get enough of them. Ah dreamt aboot the Hat, drew pictures o him and spent hoors colourin them in, hidin them under ma bed in case ma mither wid find them. Ah pestered ma faither day and night tae tell me aw aboot him and whit he got uptae.

"Well son," he wid say, "he wis a great big man, bigger and wider than oor front door. His hair wis slicked back and black as night. His face wis aw crumpled like an auld broon paper bag and his jaggy stubble pierced through it and his voice, his voice could have grated gravel. He hud the biggest honds Ah've ever seen, like shovels they wur and his fingers hud the words LOVE and HATE tattooed across them in big black letters. Often when he wis in the pub, he wid put his honds on the table, fingers spread open wide, thumb touching thumb an withoot sayin a word, the big hard men knew he meant business. It wis free drinks aw night.

"Yer Uncle Pat meant something aboot here, he could huv grown men greetin jist by lookin straight intae their eyes. He knew whit wis whit and when it wis gonny happen. Late wan night he left the hoose, he wis aw mysterious. 'Ah'm gawn tae sort oot some business,' he growled. Ah knew that meant trouble, son, and naturally Ah would huv gawn wi him but Ah hud a bit o business o ma ain."

He winked at me and nodded his heid. Ah winked back as if Ah knew whit he wis on aboot. Ah didnae but Ah couldnae let on, Ah wisnae sure why. Deep down, Ah felt disappointed and a wee bit left oot and this wis something else Ah wid come across later on in ma life.

"Anyway son," he said (his voice had become a whisper), "Pat wis on his way tae sort oot Fingers McGlone fae across the river in the Calton. This wis serious son, naebody went owr the bridge otherwise. That wis McGlone territory. Only a McVitie wid have risked this, son, coz it wis only mugs or gangsters that ventured owr there. It wis aw tae dae wi a deid body that hud turned up ootside oor local chippie. It hud nae right hond pinkie. Pat knew it hud tae be the work o the McGlone gang. He wis making his way owr the bridge and the only sound he could hear in the night wis the noise o his segs clicking oan the road below, too far away yet tae announce his arrival.

"Suddenly he saw the headlights o a motor comin towards him. He tried tae jump oot the road, but it screeched tae a halt and skidded in front o him. He stood rooted tae the spot tryin tae figure oot his next move. The doors were flung open and oot came Big Billy an Wee Wullie, their blades glistening in the street light. Next came Fingers himself, obviously no a happy man. They stood facin each other, eyes fixed. He wisnae very big but he wis awfy ugly. His face wis kinda aff-white, sometimes it even looked pale blue, and he hud a scar that zig-zagged fae wan ear to the other right across his skinny wee nose. He also had a twitch which started in his left eye, travelled doon tae the pencilled-in moustache above his mooth an finally took owr his hale heid.

→

"Big Billy and Wee Wullie circled roon yer uncle and held their knives to his throat. Fingers took oot a packet o fags and a Zippo lighter fae his pocket. He lit up, took a big draw, then blew smoke rings intae the night air. He hud gold rings oan every finger. Rings wur his trademark.

"'Ur you loast then, McVitie?' he snarled, as he poked Pat in the belly: he wisny big enough tae reach any higher. 'You know the score. You know whit's next, McVitie,' he said and suddenly yer Uncle Pat was lying sprawled across the pavement, face doon. It wis in that split second that yer uncle became Pat the Hat. His right hond pinkie wis sliced aff quick as ye like and his proud tattoo LOVE and HATE hud become LOVE and HAT. This wis like an eye-for-an-eye type of revenge, son, bit much mair serious. Ye could always get a gless eye, this wis aboot fingers. The Hat pulled himsel tae his feet and laughed. Instead o' screamin wi pain, he put oot his other hon an took back the pinkie that Fingers wis holdin. He threw back his heid and yelled, licked the blood aff the severed pinkie and threw it intae the Clyde. His laughter drowned oot the plop when it landed in the murky water on its way tae feed the fish."

It wisnae till much later when ma Uncle Pat came back fae Canada, where he'd emigrated years before Ah wis born, that Ah discovered that this legend, Pat the Hat McVitie, wis five foot four, skinny as a lollipop man's pole and aboot as dangerous. Wan thing that wis true wis he did huv the same tattoo an wan night he caught me starin at his honds and laughed. He shook his baldy heid.

"Long story, son," he said. "Ah wis working night shift in the Mother's Pride bakery slicin plain loaves when..."

Maureen Sullivan

Questions

1 List three ways in which the wee boy tries to change himself physically so that he is more like his Uncle Pat.

2 Why does he think that he might be adopted?

3 Why does the wee boy *think* his father wants to keep the stories about Pat a secret?

4 Why does his father *really* want to keep them a secret?

5 Look at the father's description of Pat. First, he compares Pat to a door: Pat is bigger and wider than the front door. List three more comparisons that the father makes.

6 What do you think the father *really* means when he says he would have gone looking for trouble with Pat, "but Ah hud a bit o business o ma ain"?

7 What impression is the father trying to give his son of the kind of man he and his brother Pat were?

8 Can you give two reasons why McGlone is called "Fingers" McGlone?

9 List three details about Finger's face and head that make him stand out.

10 How do we realise how small Fingers is compared to Pat when they meet?

11 "An eye for an eye..." type of revenge, can you complete this saying and explain what it means?

12 List three details that describe the *real* Uncle Pat. How are they different from the way the wee boy's dad described him?

13 What *really* happened to Pat's pinkie?

14 Why do you think the wee boy's dad made up such a dramatic tale?

A Closer Look at Maureen Sullivan's Writing Skills

Using exaggerated description for humour

When Maureen makes the father describe Uncle Pat, she uses exaggeration to make him larger than life. She compares him to a door, to the night, to a crumpled paper bag and to gravel. All of these exaggerate his size, the darkness of his hair, his wrinkles and the sound of his voice.

If you want to describe fantastic or dramatic characters, exaggerating what they are like can help you enormously and also entertain your readers. Think of the quality you want to describe, for example, bushy eyebrows. In reality, they might be no bushier than a large furry caterpillar, but if you compare them to something that is much much bigger and much much bushier, for example, wallpaper brushes, which are very long and wide, then you can make your writing funnier.

Creating strong characters

Maureen has created four strong characters here: the wee boy, his father, the imaginary Uncle Pat and Fingers McGlone. All of them are strongly motivated (p 44) and have strong feelings. The wee boy is obsessed with his Uncle Pat, who is his hero, and he wants to learn all he can so he can copy his hero. The father loves feeding the wee boy's imagination, and pretending at the same time that he was a hero too when he was younger. The imaginary Uncle Pat and Fingers McGlone are both gangland fighters motivated by aggression and violence.

If your characters are also highly motivated and have strong feelings, your stories will be easier to write and will work better. Try to make at least one of your characters care passionately about something.

Using imaginary heroes

We all like to have people we can look up to, people who are role models or heroes for us. We can take this idea further and come up with imaginary heroes. This is where many cartoon characters come from, like Superman or Lara Croft.

We can use the question "what if?" to create imaginary heroes. What if someone could hold their breath for a week? What if someone could jump as high as the tallest building in the world? What if an ordinary schoolchild could turn into an owl at night?

If you think of something impossible that you would love to be able to do, you are well on the way to creating an imaginary hero.

Creating a clever twist at the end

If you want to create a clever twist at the end, you have to plan carefully to set it up. You have to know what it's going to be and you have to keep that a secret from your reader until the end. Maureen knew from the start that Pat was a wee man who had an accident with a bread slicing machine. If she had told us this at the beginning of the story, it wouldn't have worked so well. However, she builds up such a huge fantasy about Pat the Hat McVitie, the gangland hero, that when we meet the real Pat at the very end, the contrast is both unexpected and entertaining.

Clever Ideas That You Can Use Too

1   Using exaggerated description for humour
2   Creating strong characters
3   Using imaginary heroes
4   Creating a clever twist at the end

Five Ideas For Your Own Writing

Idea 1

Write about an imaginary heroic aunt or uncle that you wish you had. You can start your story: "Not many people know this, but my aunt / uncle..." You can also give them a nickname related to their talent. Give this story illustrations if you wish!

Idea 2

Like Carolyn Mack, Maureen has used a proverb as inspiration for her story. Carolyn chose "All that glitters isn't gold" and she gave us only the first three words in the title assuming that we would know the rest of it.

Maureen has also given us the first half of a proverb for her title: "An eye for an eye" which is completed with "and a tooth for a tooth". This is about revenge. It is about inflicting the same kind of injuries on your attacker as they inflicted on you: it's about getting even.

Think about revenge. Is revenge a good idea? Do you think revenge can lead to peace? Is peace what we should be aiming for? How does getting your own back make you feel? How do you think it makes the other person feel? If someone attacks you, what other ways could you respond instead of hitting back? Do you think forgiveness or understanding can help?

Write down your thoughts on revenge. Write down what you think is good or bad about it. Write down what else you think people could do. Write about any experience you have had where revenge has been part of it.

Idea 3

Write a story in which someone is seeking revenge for some wrong done to them. This will involve conflict between two of your main characters. Explain the wrong that has been done (it might be a physical attack, theft, vandalism or something else). Then write about what happens when your character seeks revenge.

Idea 4

This story is about an injury, about a lost finger. There is quite an ordinary reason for this injury but Maureen writes a story in which there is a fantastic imaginary reason which turns Pat into a huge hero. Think about an injury someone might have, for which there is a perfectly ordinary explanation. Then, invent an amazing and fantastic reason for the injury in which they are a brave and daring hero.

Now write a story in which he or she, or someone else, explains the fantastic version. See if you can include a twist ending where the real version is also explained.

Idea 5

When his father winks at him and nods his head, the wee boy winks back as if he understands. But he doesn't understand and he is afraid to say so. This makes him feel left out.

Write about a time when you have pretended to understand something. Explain why you pretended and why you were afraid to ask for an explanation. What happened as a result of you pretending to understand?

If you prefer, you can write this as a story about someone else and make up something they pretend to understand. You can make the results of their misunderstanding as serious as you want!

Links between "All That Glitters" and "An Eye for an Eye"

Please make sure you have read both of these stories before you read any further.

Both Carolyn Mack and Maureen Sullivan have used proverbs to give them the titles and the ideas for their stories.

Look again at the first sentence of each story (p 158 / p 171). As we saw in the section on openings (p 53), both of them have very strong openings which make us want to read on.

Angels are supposed to be good creatures but, in Carolyn's story, she turns this idea on its head and gives us the opposite: an angel who has done something wrong and who is to blame.

In Maureen's story, we have a legend, but only in one room, which turns the idea of a legend around.

Both stories start with children who are obsessed by something. What is each child obsessed with?

Both stories are also about a child who is deceived. How is the child in "All That Glitters" deceived? How is the child in "An Eye for an Eye" deceived?

Both stories also end with a child who becomes older and wiser.

Both stories have used powerful description twice: once at the start when the child was deceived, and again near the end, when the child realises the truth.

Both use exaggeration to make their stories more entertaining.

These are all useful skills for a writer:

writing a good opening

using a proverb as inspiration

including obsession and deception

writing powerful description

using exaggeration for humour.

There is one more skill, which you can find in these two stories.

This is where the writer sets up an expectation and then gives us the opposite. So, the angel doll in "All That Glitters" is set up to be wonderful but ends up the complete opposite. Pat the Hat is set up to be a giant of a gangster hero, but ends up the opposite: a skinny, little, bald man who worked in a bread factory.

You will also find the idea of opposites being used by Ted Hughes in the next poem.

Using opposites can help us create powerful and entertaining writing.

Picture 11

Use this picture to inspire you to write a story or a poem or a memory or a hope.

You can write about it in whatever way you wish, but it might help you to think about the following 8 questions. (There are no wrong answers...)

1 What does this seem to be?
2 What else might it be?
3 Who or what might be connected to this?
4 Where might it be?
5 When?
6 Who or what else might be involved?
7 What could happen next?
8 What sounds, smells or feelings could there be?

Chapter 22

Moon-Ravens

Before reading "Moon-Ravens"

Before we look at this poem, let's think a little about the colours black and white.

First, what does the colour black make you think of? Would you say black is usually associated with good or bad things?

Second, what does the colour white make you think of? Would you say white is usually associated with good or bad things?

Can you think of any black animals or birds or insects?

Can you think of any white animals or birds or insects?

What is a raven? See how much you can find out about where they live and what they eat and whether they are thought to be good luck or bad luck. (See p 186–187 if you're stuck...)

The title of the poem we are going to look at is "Moon-Ravens". Given what you now know about ravens, can you predict what a moon-raven might be like? What colour might it be? What kind of sound might it make? What time of day might you see one? What kind of magical powers might it have?

Now read the poem, at least twice, and aloud.

Moon-Ravens

Are silver white
Like moonlight
And their croak, their bark
Is not dark
And ominous,
But luminous
And a sweet chime
Always announcing time
For good news to come
If there is some,
And if there isn't
Then there's a moon-present –
That is, a stillness,
And if you have any illness
It flits out of your mouth
In the shape of a black moth

Which the moon-raven then follows
And swallows.

Ted Hughes

Questions

1   What do you notice about the rhyming scheme (p 37) in this poem? How many half-rhymes can you find?

2   What do you notice about the way the title connects to the poem?

3   How many sentences are in the poem?

4   Why do you think Ted has left a gap before the last two lines?

5   Why do you think he has made the last line so short?

6   How does this poem make you feel?

7   Would you like a moon-raven as a pet? Why, or why not?

A Closer Look at Ted Hughes' Writing Skills

Creating opposites

Ted has created opposites here: a black bird has become a silver-white bird; a daytime bird has become a night bird with moons and moths; and a bird that was associated with death has instead become a healing bird.

By changing what we normally expect into the opposite, we can create unusual situations or creatures.

Using the idea of sympathetic magic

Sympathetic magic is the idea that if you do something good (or bad) to a representation of someone, then the good (or bad) will actually happen to them. We tend to know of sympathetic magic only as a bad force, like voodoo dolls, where if someone sticks a pin in a doll's stomach, then the real person represented by the doll is supposed to get a pain in their stomach.

But, sympathetic magic can also work for good, as in "Moon-Ravens". Here, the illness is transformed into a moth and swallowed by the healing moon-raven.

Ted is using ideas from different cultures, religions and legends as a springboard for his poem.

Using soft consonants and long vowels

Ted has given his poem a soothing and peaceful sound by using words with soft, slow consonants like "m… n… l… s…" and by using long vowel sounds like "oo… a… oa… o…" which make the music of the poem smooth and flowing.

Read the poem aloud and listen carefully to the sounds you are making. Can you write down six words from the poem which use soft, slow consonants and/or long vowels? If you are aware of the effect the *sound* of words can have on our feelings, then you too can choose words not only for their meaning, but for their sound too.

Running the title into the poem

Most poems have a title which comes before the poem itself starts. With "Moon-Ravens", Ted has used the title as the first word of a sentence which continues with the rest of the poem. This makes the poem flow more smoothly because we don't pause after reading the title.

If we did this all the time, it would become boring and predictable. If we do this occasionally, it makes our poems more unusual.

Clever Ideas That You Can Use Too

1   Creating opposites
2   Using the idea of sympathetic magic
3   Using soft consonants and long vowels
4   Running the title into the poem

Two Ideas For Your Own Writing

Idea 1

Think of four creatures where their colour is important. List them.

Choose the one you find most unusual or interesting.

Decide whether it is seen as lucky or unlucky.

Then, as in "Moon-Ravens", change the colours and the kind of luck and the name. Think of opposites...

You might want to make a creature of the day become a creature of the night... or a night creature become a day creature.

Give it a new name.

Discuss and make notes on the appearance, sound, smell, movement, habitat, behaviour and magical powers that your new creature has.

Using "Moon-Ravens" as a model, if you wish, draft a poem selecting ideas from your notes. Try to use some of the writing skills you have seen Ted use in "Moon-Ravens". Listen to the *sounds* of the words you are using.

Edit and redraft your poem until you are happy with it.

You might also like to sketch the creature and its habitat, and the good or evil deeds it can do.

Idea 2

Imagine you have a moon-raven as a secret pet. How did you get it? Where do you keep it? How do you feed it? What is its name? Someone you love gets ill. How can you help them? Write the story of what happens.

Ravens: Fact and Fantasy

The raven is the biggest bird in the crow family, which also includes carrion crows, rooks and hooded crows. It is an enormous bird, all black, longer than a buzzard, and with a similar wingspan reaching 130 cm wide. It lives in remote places, like moorland and islands, on the West of Scotland. It eats carrion, which is dead flesh. Its call is a harsh "cronck-cronck". (This information comes from *Collins Bird Guide*, HarperCollins, 2001.)

Because it is big and black and not very pretty, and because it eats dead things, people have created legends around it. Some believe that ravens can foretell death, illness and bad luck. Others believe that ravens can predict bad weather because they leave the area before it arrives.

An ancient legend from Rome tells of a time when ravens were handsome, big, white birds, like swans. The Roman god, Apollo, was in love with a nymph called Coronis. However, Coronis preferred someone else, and the raven – the beautiful, big, white raven – told Apollo this. Apollo was furious and shot Coronis and turned the raven into an ugly, black bird as punishment for being the bringer of bad news.

Ravens aren't always considered bad luck. The Tower of London has ravens as guardians. Elijah, the Old Testament prophet, and Saint Paul, the hermit, were both fed by ravens when they were in the desert. There are also old paintings of saints with ravens: St Oswald has a tame raven on his hand which has a ring in its mouth, and St Benedict has a raven standing at his feet.

This information about legends surrounding ravens comes from *Brewer's Dictionary of Phrase and Fable*, which is a fascinating book. It can give you not only information but ideas for writing too.

Can you find out anything else about ravens from any other sources?

Picture 12

Use this picture to inspire you to write a story or a poem or a memory or a hope.

You can write about it in whatever way you wish, but it might help you to think about the following 8 questions. (There are no wrong answers…)

1 What does this seem to be?

2 What else might it be?

3 Who or what might be connected to this?

4 Where might it be?

5 When?

6 Who or what else might be involved?

7 What could happen next?

8 What sounds, smells or feelings could there be?

Chapter 23

Fahim 911

My hands were slippery. I wiped them on my dragon T-shirt. I didn't want her to know I was excited. She squeezed my hand really, really tight.

"It's going to be all right," her voice wasn't like my real mummy. My mummy had a sing-song voice.

She pulled me over to where the policeman had tripped the man up. He slept on the road. The policeman asked him to put his hands behind his head. But I don't think he could hear. He didn't move. It was too noisy, the yellow taxi cabs beeped a lot and the buses farted too! I was worried the big police horses might trample on the man. The policemen on horses kept all the people moving.

One of the policemen looked at me and whispered to her. I can read lips. I have to read Daddy's lips: he's always too far away.

"Do you know that man, Ma'am?"

"No."

She sounded like she was about to cry. I thought maybe I should cry too. I wanted to see the man's face.

"Did the man grab your son or not?"

"Yes, I think so."

He didn't grab me.

"Ma'am, please, this is a very serious accusation, can you be more specific?"

She saw me run.

"Officer, I adopted Fahim two years ago after his father died in the attacks on 911. Fahim thinks he sees his father."

→

People look at me funny when they think my daddy disappeared.

"So your son thinks that's his father?"

"He ran after the man and held his hand. The man started to walk away with Fahim."

A lady policeman stood with me, she rubbed her gun. It was black but not shiny.

I did try not to run like when I saw Daddy last time. I didn't run. He told me to stay with my new mummy. He put his finger over his mouth to tell me hush! He always told me to keep quiet so my new family liked me. Sometimes I listened to him and stayed quiet but I think my new mum wants a too-much-talking-child. She worries if I stay quiet.

We were going to put flowers where Daddy used to work. A lot of other people must have lost their daddies too because there were lots of flowers on the street and people crying.

The policeman came over to me.

"You think you can answer some questions for me?"

His voice was scratchy.

"OK."

A helicopter flew really low down.

"Do you recognize this man?"

"I don't know."

He took me to where the man was.

"That's not my dad."

"Did you see your dad today?"

My new mum looked really, really worried. I wanted her to be happy.

"No, I didn't."

She smiled.

They took the man away.

We lined up to light a candle even though it was still sunny. When I got to the front of the queue, Daddy helped me light mine. We warmed our hands in the flame. He winked at me.

Evelyn Jean-Louis

Questions

1 How do we know, from paragraph 1, that this story is from the point of view of a child?

2 Why does Fahim not want her to know that he is excited?

3 What one word in the second paragraph tells us that his real mummy is no longer alive?

4 Why do you think he isn't looking for his mummy, in the same way as he is looking for his daddy?

5 Fahim can see his daddy's face. Why do you think he can no longer hear his daddy's voice?

6 Why do you think Fahim thought he should cry too if his new mum were going to cry?

7 Why is Fahim caught between what his daddy wants and what his new mum wants?

8 Do you think Fahim knows himself what he wants? What are your reasons for thinking this?

9 Fahim tells the policeman he didn't see his father because he wants his new mum to be happy. What do you think is the truth? Why might it make her unhappy?

10 Fahim's daddy is still alive for him. What do you think his daddy means when he winks at Fahim at the end?

11 Fahim is missing his daddy so much that he imagines he sees him and runs after men who might be him. He tries to keep this a secret from his new mum. How do you think she feels towards Fahim?

12 What age do you think Fahim is? Why do you think this?

13 In the second paragraph, his new mum says, "It's going to be all right". Do you think it is going to be all right? Why do you think this?

→

14 911 is an American way of noting dates. This means the 11th
    day of the 9th month, that is, the 11th of September. On this
    day in 2001, terrorists flew two planes into two skyscraper office
    blocks, known as the Twin Towers, in New York. The huge
    towers both collapsed in flames and nearly 3000 people died.
    Most of the bodies were never found. If you didn't already know
    this, what details does Evelyn give you that could help you work
    it out from the story?

15 How much do you need to know about 911, in order to
    understand the story?

A Closer Look at Evelyn Jean-Louis's Writing Skills

Creating a child character

Evelyn creates a very believable child character here. She does
this in two ways: by using simple sentences and by giving us the
details that a child would notice.

Look at the first paragraph. The sentences are very short and
simple. The details in them, the dragon T-shirt and holding
someone's hand, tell us that this is a child. Evelyn also tells us
that Fahim is trying to keep his excitement a secret. Secrets are
important in this story.

Evelyn continues to use short simple sentences all through the
story. She also continues to write about childlike details that
Fahim notices, for example, the noises of the taxi cabs and buses,
the policemen, the horses, the gun and the helicopter.

Evelyn is able to see the world from Fahim's point of view (p 39)
and to write about it as if she were as young as he is. This is
something you too can do, when you write from someone else's
point of view. Think not only about what they would see and
hear and feel, but how they would write about it.

Turning expectations on their head

Evelyn makes her story more interesting because she gives us the opposite of what we would expect. For example, it is more likely that a grown-up would try to kidnap a child, than that a child would run up to a stranger and take their hand. Also, when people die, we don't see them again but, two years after his death, Fahim can still "see" his father.

If you think about what people will expect, and then turn that idea on its head, you can come up with good writing. We have seen opposites being used in the previous three pieces of writing too: "All That Glitters", "An Eye for an Eye" and "Moon-Ravens".

Using secrets

Fahim cannot accept that he won't see his father again. So he lives in a world where his father is still alive but he has to keep this a secret. Instead of telling the truth, he says what he thinks people want to hear. This means that the people who would like to help him, like his new mum and the policeman, are not able to get close to him.

Secrets are very useful when you're writing a story. They generate conflict between the person who has the secret and others who would like to know it.

Creating a bittersweet ending

Bittersweet means something that is both bitter and sweet at the same time, like a slice of lemon with sugar on it. In this story, the ending is bittersweet because it is both happy and sad. It is happy because Fahim's new mum thinks he didn't see his daddy after all, and that this means he is beginning to accept that his father has gone. It is also happy because Fahim's daddy helps him to light the candle, which makes Fahim very happy.

However, the ending is sad too because Fahim is keeping a big secret from his new mum and is still living in a world where he believes his father is still alive.

Endings like this are very effective. Writing about secrets can help you create a bittersweet ending.

Clever Ideas That You Can Use Too

1   Creating a child character

2   Turning expectations on their head

3   Using secrets

4   Creating a bittersweet ending

Three Ideas for Your Own Writing

Idea 1

This is a ghost story about a child who "sees" his dead father. Write your own ghost story about a parent or grandparent who "sees" their lost child or grandchild. Decide whether they keep this a secret or not. If not, how do others react to them? Decide what makes the ghost appear. For Fahim, it is seeing a man who, from behind, reminds him of his father. But a ghost could appear as a result of an object, a sound, smell, a movement...

Idea 2

"Fahim 911" is a gentle ghost story about a grieving young orphan who is trying hard to pretend that he is happy with his new mum and not missing his daddy. Near the end, he lies to the policeman when he says he didn't see his daddy.

Pick up the story starting with the question, "Did you see your dad today?" and continue it, with Fahim instead giving open and honest answers. See if you can work towards a happier ending, where Fahim no longer feels he has to try to make his new mum happy.

Idea 3

Fahim is keeping a big secret from everyone. Write a story about a big secret someone (you?) has to try to keep and about what happens when it escapes. Try to create a bittersweet ending that is both happy and sad.

Picture 13

Use this picture to inspire you to write a story or a poem or a memory or a hope.

You can write about it in whatever way you wish, but it might help you to think about the following 8 questions. (There are no wrong answers...)

1   What does this seem to be?

2   What else might it be?

3   Who or what might be connected to this?

4   Where might it be?

5   When?

6   Who or what else might be involved?

7   What could happen next?

8   What sounds, smells or feelings could there be?

Chapter 24

A Symbol of Hope

A Symbol of Hope

Mrs Gallagher's Class, P7, had just returned from an exciting trip to the Magilligan Field Centre. One of the boys, Michael, was strangely silent and thoughtful: he was thinking about the Nature Museum in the Centre and in particular a cross-section of a large tree which clearly showed many rings. Each of these, they had been told, represented a year of the tree's life. Someone had tagged each ring with a date and an event which had occurred on that date. Trees have seen so much, thought Michael, that they really can tell the past.

But Michael was never one for thinking of one thing for too long and soon, while tucking into a second helping of his mum's stew, he had nothing more on his mind than the next day's fishing trip. His mum had his sandwiches in the fridge and his wellingtons and rod were at the back door, so all that remained for him to do was collect his bait.

Early next morning, armed with his bait and his rod, he set off to the nearby River Foyle where he found his favourite spot. After baiting his hook and casting his line, he settled down to the serious job of waiting.

→

Suddenly Michael jumped to his feet: he thought he had heard something. He listened. No, it wasn't that he had heard something: he realised that what had startled him was the complete silence. The birds made no sound, there was no rustling of leaves and even the water was still. It was as though time had stopped. Michael tried to run but his legs were frozen. Now he knew what was meant by the expression, "Your heart is in your mouth". How he wished he was safely back in his bedroom.

Michael felt a strong presence. He looked around. There was nothing there, except the river, the grass and the trees. That's it, thought Michael, TREES!

Michael was drawn to an oak tree. Under its shady branches he closed his eyes. His head was filled with a million sounds and lights. He felt the world about him changing. Opening his eyes he looked around: everything had changed. The river was still there, but further away. The river bank was steeper and where the oak tree had stood now stood a sapling. Michael felt very frightened and alone. He felt he was living through a nightmare and all he wanted to do was to waken up and find himself safely at home in his own bedroom. Michael knew where the tree had taken him to, but not which period of time. Time had in some way changed.

Where the road had been was now a mucky path. As Michael climbed it, a strange smell hit him. It was a strange odour which

Michael had never experienced before. It was so bad it made him feel like being sick. What on earth was it? Holding a handkerchief over his mouth and nose he continued to climb to the top of the path.

In front of him was a large barren field covered in a black sticky slime. Here and there, stick-like objects, which he knew at one time must have been plants, stuck out of the ground.

The stench was almost unbearable and just as Michael turned to run away, he caught sight of a small group of people, a man and two children, or at least he thought it was two children. The man was tall and thin and the skin on his face was so stretched it looked like a mask. The second figure was a woman but she was so small and shrunken that Michael had mistaken her for a child. The child looked like E.T. with a large head and big hollow eyes which filled his face. He just stared into space. His arms hung by his sides as though they were not part of his body. He had a huge stomach and Michael thought that at least he was well fed.

Then it dawned on him that he had seen children like this before in pictures of an Ethiopian Famine. He had done a project in school on the Famine in Ireland and the Potato Blight of 1845. He had read about the hunger and the smell, but it was nothing like this. He remembered how he had been told that rotation of crops could have helped and how grain and food were being exported from ports in Ireland.

He ran forward to tell them, but they couldn't see or hear him. He only existed in a different time. Michael was filled with many emotions: frustration, anger, fear, sadness and guilt.

The man and woman worked quietly, digging in the ground, while the strange child just stood there. The man then spoke in a language that was different, yet somehow familiar. It was Irish. Michael had learned a little in school but he knew no more than a few words. He was no longer surprised when he found that he could understand everything they said. He just accepted it as part of the strange thing that was happening to him.

When the people got up to go he decided to follow them. Then the man turned back and told the woman and child to wait. He made his way down the path to the oak sapling, he scraped the earth around it and stuck a strong stick in the ground alongside it to give it support. It was obvious that the tree meant a lot to him but it was all very weird.

Their house, when they got there, was a one-roomed, thatched cottage with a low door. It had one tiny window. Michael entered the smoke-filled room. The smoke came from a small fire which burned at one end of the room. It somehow found its way up the wall and out of a small hole in the roof. There was no chimney. The furniture consisted of a table, two stools and a bed which was separated from the rest of the room by a curtain. The only other thing in the room was a large box.

Feeling like an intruder but wanting to know more about this family that he felt somehow part of, he sat on the box and watched as the woman, whose name he learnt was Brid, took water from an iron pot on the fire and gently washed the boy. When he heard the child's name a shiver ran through him. It was Miceal, which is Irish for Michael. This was something else which tied him to the family. The father, Ruarai, talked quietly about the future and how they would survive. They had a home, each other and a lot of love. He told them how the oak sapling was sprouting more and more branches and, as it would grow and survive, so would they. Once again Michael tried to communicate but it was no use.

He felt their pain and suffering was too much, so he left their home, and made his way back to the tree, crying all the way. He felt it was so hopeless and that it was an awful waste. Then he looked at the young tree: it was standing straight and firm. Its leaves and branches were fresh and green and, as he had come from its future, he knew it had survived. It was their symbol of hope.

A great weight lifted from him as he sat down beside the tree and closed his eyes. Again he experienced the strange sensation of his head being filled with a million sounds and lights and he knew that he was going forward again in time.

It was all still. He opened his eyes and he was back. Nothing had changed: the great oak stood before him once more. The river flowed gently on, his rod and line were still there and so were his uneaten sandwiches.

Michael spent a lot of time in his room after that and worried his mum by his lack of appetite.

At first he was afraid to go back to the tree but when he did get the courage to go back, the tree was gone – taken away in the name of progress. He told no one about what had happened but he read a lot about the famine and the history of that time. When he was older he wrote a poem about his experience and, when he found, while tracing his family tree, that six generations back he had had great, great, great, great-grandparents called Ruarai and Brid who had one son called Miceal, he wasn't in the least surprised.

John McDaid

(When John wrote this story, he was at primary school. He was at St Brigid's Primary School in Londonderry, in Northern Ireland. This story won him First Prize in the very first Pushkin Prizes Creative Writing Competition in Northern Ireland in 1988.)

Questions

1 In the second paragraph, John mentions food several times. List three kinds of food here.

2 These might seem like unimportant details at this point in the story, but, now that you have read the whole story, why is food so important?

3 What is the first sign, in paragraph 4, that Michael's world is changing?

4 What do you think the "strong presence" is?

5 Why do you think our bedrooms seem such safe places?

6 In what ways are the river, the tree and the road different in the past?

Questions continued

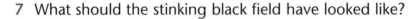

7 What should the stinking black field have looked like?

8 Why does Michael think, at first, that the woman is a child?

9 Why does Michael think, at first, that the child is well fed?

10 What does he then realise?

11 Michael lists five emotions that he feels, when he realises he can't communicate with them. They are: frustration, anger, fear, sadness and guilt. Choose three of these and explain why Michael feels each one.

12 Michael has been surprised by all the things that have happened to him so far. Why is he no longer surprised when he finds he can understand Irish?

13 Why does the man turn back to the oak sapling?

14 Why does Ruarai believe they will survive?

15 When Michael realises that the tree is a symbol of hope, he feels a great weight has been lifted from him and he can return to the present. Can you explain why this is?

16 Why do you think Michael eats less after his visit to the past?

17 When Michael goes back, the tree is gone, "in the name of progress". Michael doesn't seem bothered by this. Why do you think this is?

18 Why does Michael tell no one about what happened to him?

19 Why do we use the word "tree" for our family's past?

20 Why is Michael not surprised to learn he had met his ancestors from six generations back?

21 Why do you think this meeting with his ancestors happened in the first place?

A Closer Look at John McDaid's Writing Skills

Planting ideas

Near the beginning of this story, John plants two ideas which don't seem very important at the time, but which become important as the story develops. For example, at the end of his first paragraph, he plants the idea of trees being able to tell the past. His second paragraph tells us there is plenty of food for Michael. Both of these ideas become very important later on in the story.

Using senses

Sound (or the lack of it) is important in this story. John also uses smell powerfully when he writes about the disgusting smell of the field.

Using emotions

There are lots of emotions in this story. Michael is the character who experiences most of them, although he also gives us enough information about the family for us to guess at how they were feeling too.

Shifting between the world of the present and the world of the past

When writers want characters to move from one world to another, there is usually some kind of "doorway". In this story, the doorway is Michael closing his eyes, feeling the world changing around him and sensing strange sounds and lights. Can you think of any other stories (on paper, film or TV) where there is a different kind of doorway into another world?

Using a symbol

The title of this story is "A Symbol of Hope". In it, the oak sapling is more than just a tree. Its young healthy life in the midst of famine and death gives Ruarai hope that his son will not die in the famine, but that the family will continue down the generations. So, the health of the tree and the health of his family become connected. In this way, the tree is used as a symbol of hope.

We will return to the idea of symbols in the section on ideas for your own writing.

Clever Ideas That You Can Use Too

1   Planting ideas

2   Using senses

3   Using emotions

4   Shifting between the world of the present and the world of the past

5   Using a symbol

Eight Ideas for Your Own Writing

Idea 1

"When he was older, he wrote a poem about his experience...". Can you write Michael's poem about meeting his ancestors during the famine? Remember to use your senses, particularly sight, smell and sound.

Idea 2

Michael was fascinated when he learnt about the rings trees have within their trunks. See if you can research how these rings are formed and how they can reveal weather patterns in the past. See if you can also research how old trees can become. Can you find out where the oldest living tree in Scotland is? Can you find out where the tallest tree in Scotland is and what kind of tree it is? Can you find out where the biggest hedge in Scotland is? Can you find out where there is a whole fossilised tree standing upright in the face of a cliff on a Scottish island? Can you find out how many million years old it is? Write down anything else interesting you find out about trees during your research.

Idea 3

John's story is based on a historical event. See if you can find out why the Irish potato crop failed so badly in 1845. John mentions "rotation of crops". Can you find out what this means? See if you can also find out why grain and food were being exported during a time of famine. Where was it going to?

Also, see if you can find out about a potato famine in Scotland at the same time.

Idea 4

Write a story in which you travel back into the past and encounter one of your ancestors. It might be someone who has passed down to you a skill that you have, or it might be someone who can explain about that unusual object in your house that has been handed down through several generations and about which no one can remember the truth any more.

Idea 5

If you have studied a particular period in history, write a story set in that time and place. You can travel back to that time and that place yourself, as Michael does in John's story, or else you can write a story about a young person who is living through the historical events you have learned about.

Idea 6

John's story is called "A Symbol of Hope". Here, the tree is a symbol of hope because it can survive the famine and blight.

Some symbols are widely recognised. For example, a white dove symbolises peace because white is considered to be the colour of goodness, purity and peace, and doves are gentle-looking birds. Can you imagine the ostrich of peace instead? Or the eagle of peace? What do these two birds normally symbolise?

(If you have looked at Ted Hughes' poem, "Moon-Ravens" (p 182), you will be familiar with the symbolism we attach to the colours black and white. If you have looked at Anne MacLeod's poem, "Easter Eggs" (p 117), you will be familiar with the symbolism of Easter eggs.)

See if you can write a story in which a creature or object is used as a symbol. It can be a symbol of something good or bad.

Idea 7

Try to draw up your own family tree. Start with you and any brothers and sisters, then your two parents, each with their brothers and sisters, then four grandparents, again with brothers and sisters, then eight great-grandparents...

Idea 8

When Michael goes back to see the tree for the last time, he finds that it has been "taken away in the name of progress". Do you think that cutting down trees is progress? Can you think of three good reasons for cutting down trees? Can you think of three bad reasons for cutting down trees? Do you think we are looking after our world properly? How would you like the world to be when you grow up?

Links between "Fahim 911" and "A Symbol of Hope"

Please make sure you have read both of these stories before you read any further.

Gentle ghosts and communication difficulties

Both of these stories are ghost stories, with the child as the main character who is related to the ghost or ghosts.

All the ghosts are gentle rather than frightening. Neither Fahim nor Michael can speak to the ghosts, although they want to. Fahim is able to understand what his ghost father means by reading his lips, but he can't hear his voice or say anything back to him. Although Michael can see and hear his ghost ancestors, they cannot see or hear him at all: they do not even know he is there.

So, if you are writing a ghost story, you can choose how much or how little communication there is between your main character and the ghosts. You can also choose to make your ghosts disturbing and scary, or gentle ghosts. How different would these two stories have been, if the ghosts had been scary?

Secrets

Secrets are important in both of these stories. Fahim is trying to keep it a secret that he still sees his father and Michael doesn't tell anyone about seeing his ghost ancestors.

What impact does keeping these secrets have on the way both boys behave towards others? To help you answer this, look at the paragraph in "Fahim 911" which begins, "I did not try to run like when I saw Daddy last time..." (p 190) and also look at the second last paragraph (p 201) in "A Symbol of Hope".

The past

Both ghosts come from the past, and Fahim's ghost is only a few years old, but Michael's ghosts are from six generations before him. We know that Michael sees his ghost ancestors just once. Do you think Fahim will continue to see his ghost father? Do you think the way he sees him might change? How? Why?

Time-travel

When Michael visits his ancestors who were alive long before him, he is travelling back in time. Would you say Fahim is travelling through time to see his father?

Often, in writing that includes time-travel or ghosts, it is not easy to speak with those from another time.

If you like to read writing that crosses into a different time, you might enjoy a novel called *Tom's Midnight Garden* by Philippa Pearce. Philippa handles time-travel and another world, that of the midnight garden, extremely well.

"Rules" for Ghost Stories

If we were to try to make up "rules" for ghost stories, what would they be? Think about the following eleven statements and decide if they are true or false.

Of course, there are no correct answers because we are creating ideas, but thinking about possible answers will help you to understand how you can use ghosts in your stories.

1   Ghosts have to be frightening.

2   Only one character in a story can see the ghost.

3   If everyone can see the ghost, then it's not a ghost.

4   Ghosts must be people or animals who have died.

5   Ghosts have messages for us.

6   Ghosts must go away eventually.

7   Ghosts must be unhappy.

8   Ghosts cannot be touched.

9   Ghosts are always white.

10   Ghosts have no smell.

11   Ghosts cannot make noises.

Time-travel in "Zoo" and "A Symbol of Hope"

Please make sure you have read these two stories before you read any further.

Both stories include travel through time.

In "Zoo", Edward D. Hoch has decided to set his story in the future. He hasn't given us a particular date, but we know it is the future because interplanetary travel is possible.

In "A Symbol of Hope", we also have time-travel, but backwards into the past by six generations when Michael visits his ancestors.

The difference is that the first story is set in the future and all the action happens in that time, so the time-travel has taken place before the story begins. How is the time-travel different in "A Symbol of Hope"?

If you've thought about the difference, you should now be able to see that you can either set your *whole* story in a different time, past or future, or else you can make a character travel in time, *within* your story. They can travel either back into the past, or forwards into the future.

Picture 14

Use this picture to inspire you to write a story or a poem or a memory or a hope.

You can write about it in whatever way you wish, but it might help you to think about the following 8 questions. (There are no wrong answers...)

1   What does this seem to be?

2   What else might it be?

3   Who or what might be connected to this?

4   Where might it be?

5   When?

6   Who or what else might be involved?

7   What could happen next?

8   What sounds, smells or feelings could there be?